PETER JEFFERY OAM

First published in Australia by HiveMind Press 2022.

Copyright © HiveMind Press, 2022.

Peter Jeffery OAM has asserted his moral right under the Copyright Act 1968, [2006], and Patents Act 1990, to be identified as the author of this work.

All rights reserved. No reproduction, copy or transmission of this publication may be made without written permission. No paragraph of this publication may be reproduced, copied or transmitted save with written permission or in accordance with the provisions of the Copyright Act 1968, [2006]. Any person who does any unauthorised act in relation to this publication may be liable to criminal prosecution and civil claims for damages.

ISBN: 9780646803470

Typeset/Cover Design by - HiveMind Press.

A GENERAL MUCH TIRED OF WAR

PETER JEFFERY OAM

Dedication

For Lou Klepac and my long-suffering wife Julie Evans who is my constant support through the triumphs and vicissitudes of as the Chinese wryly say, 'my long and interesting life!'.

Introduction

Some of the readers who are old enough to remember when they learned poems by heart as part of the curriculum, and since, have carried that skill all through their lives, whereas current students are more likely to be involved with a film script than with a poem.

For some of my generation they saw it as a chore and equally reluctant teachers 'got it over and done with !'

Whereas the lucky others of us had fire breathing poetry evangelists for mentors. They showed us that we could make poems a vital and necessary part of our whole life. We learned that poetry breathed along with life and applied its wisdom in almost proverb like phrases and allusions for the many changing circumstances we came across.

Which brings me to the title of my book A GENERAL MUCH TIRED OF WAR, for it was my 'wanderjahr' friend the celebrated deputy director of the Art Gallery of WA Lou Klepac and the formidable publisher of benchmark art books featuring many of Australia's greatest artists such as Nolan, Drysdale, Cassab, and Whitely with his Beagle Press who was one of the two people who on blessed occasions could recite a poem of mine verbatim, and by doing so made it part of their mindscape as much as it had been mine. In his case it was for my General.

So when my second book TRUE TO POETRY IN MY FASHION appeared he thumbed through it looking for his favourite and was chagrined that the General did not appear and duly reprimanded me for it. Hence when I had assembled this my next book of verse and presentations it was a delight to entitle it thus A GENERAL MUCH TIRED OF WAR and to dedicate it to him and my wife Julie, who you will see has a section devoted solely to her elsewhere in the book.

The other person was David Hough, who is known for his masterful historical accounts of His Majesty's Theatre and Boans our great emporium, and his delightful obituaries alongside Patrick Cornish in the WEST AUSTRALIAN of significant West Australians from all walks of life. His poem was the poem FIVE I SPENT which involved Judas and the five senses and his thirty pieces of silver, in the tenor of a religious folk song.

In its early history, poetry - as recited by the bards - was the archival repository of all tribal knowledge as can be seen with say, the genealogy of ruling leaders; cartography of cultural migration; details of both astronomy and astrology; history as marked by battles and massacres; folk medical prescriptions; canons of permissible social and sexual relations; 'ur' or foundation mythology In short, almost anything that could be uttered and that needed its recording, before myth hardened into history, and folklore consolidated as the scientific disciplines.

My haphazard Collected and Selected verse, utilises poetry for its great diversity and flexibility, to marry in with many genres and formats and different art forms. It might be regarded by the reader as a curate's egg because of it diverse presentations. Hopefully, s/he will revel in what sections of verse appeal , and forebear its excesses as experimentation and sentimental indulgence wrenched by sad circumstance and immediate expression.

For a long time I had envied the many poets who had their poems made into songs, so I am thrilled that recent TOM COLLIN'S PRIZE winner Mike Greenacre converted my crude cathouse rap or blues 'Liza, Liza, I hear yah knockin'!' into an enjoyable gift. One will see that I write longish imagistic elegies as several dear friends pass. And my proudest moment of collaboration is with Arthur Gracias and his superb interplay of Indo-jazz fusion with my verse cycle 'Desert Dying' dedicated to the Afghan camel drivers. Because of my poor mnemonic skills I generally perform with the reading of a printed text, but recently ventured into two performance pieces. Here and there I satirise in short sharp verses and of tenor between vulgar and elevated.

Foreword for A General Much Tired of War

The smoke has cleared. The enemy is scattered. But this is not the final victory; there never will be a final victory; the enemy will regroup and before long lay siege on the territory he has gained. Younger officers seek promotion with the promise that they will finish the job with one bold stroke. He is due for retirement, they say; a ceremonial old age of official speeches, ribbon cutting and high teas with VIPs. He doesn't hold it against them; he said much the same thing in his youth. But no one knows the terrain like him, nor the wicked wiles and stratagems of this implacable enemy. When he was young he vowed he would fight to the death. But now he is a general much tired of war.

The enemy is indifference. And in this vast and lonely land there is no foe more persistent. It attacks from all sides. It whispers into the ears of bureaucrats and politicians the default go-to for cuts and cost savings making cultural venues and other platforms disappear. It seizes his own motivation making him succumb to a torpor of pointlessness. The fight against this enemy is neverending. Defending the first front requires tireless marshalling, committee sitting and cheerfulness. Attacking on the second front entails overcoming himself; for he, as a West Australian, is made from the very stuff of his enemy. In him it is a shapelessness that must be concentrated into a unique verse of long, stepped syntax and enormous vocabulary. Herein is a record of this fight of 70 years, for consolidation and legacy are now uppermost in his mind and he is a general much tired of war.

These are the despatches from his many campaigns in solitude. They tell the life-journey from a romantic young versifier in the decade after the Second World War to the thundering, stumbling master, commander of the English language, that he is today. Through the prism of his journey they tell the cultural history of the state of Western Australia, the fields on which he, and others, have fought for a vibrant civic and intellectual life. And what an epic of activism and thought they tell. There isn't a single sense or mood that is not touched by these lines. Most immediate is their physicality. We see his unruly body in the overflow of the lines; images spring to my mind as I think of them   his eyes red and puffy with hayfever, his big knees jammed against a backrest in a cinema, his big relaxed hands pushing the beautiful spidery lines out with a pen; the overflow, the outside, where his body is, all realised pungently in this verse. But this is an adventure of the mind too, for out there is the world that he has lived and fought in over seven decades. All of his vast reading in philosophy, history, and fiction, all of his observations during travel are brought to bear on the world with insights that are piercing, restlessly intellectual, and full of joy. What a loss this state will suffer when he leaves us.

But for now he still commands the field. His unflagging can-do energy, his capacity to attend to multiple engagements, to listen and respond to many competing voices with a magnanimous and yet singular focus, and his wicked worldly laughter at all the silly clevernesses that he recognises in us younger officers, are still familiar at so many cultural battlefronts in Perth. How much have we come to depend on his presence? For he is not superhuman; he is a mortal man, and lately has begun to hint to me, in asides, and in ever new poems, that he is a general much tired of war.

Chris Palazzolo
Kununurra, 2021

A General Much Tired of War

They watch me in the field,
load my cannon, wheel my squadrons of horse,
scribble with jewelled fingers my warring maps, and
now that we rest, they come to me with talk.

We will give
a Medici palace, title, and wife.
all these will we give
for thy banner a year on the Tuscan plains,

I watch their eager eyes,
and as I speak, their noble lips quiver,

I am going home, signori,
to the Christ-twisted vines,
to the white chapped fountain,
and to the wheat gold stubble on the brown earth's
chin.

[...]

For these are my blood;
but now my heart.
she is proud,
like a tall pine in high winds;
she is soft,
like deep snow freshly fallen;
and she is beauty,
like spring fruit, sudden burst or flamed.

These things she is;
and she is mine, signori.

She waits,
and my horse is saddled.
I ride no more in the chalk white dust,
I ride in stars and meteors shower my way.

They bend from the wait, speak polite regret,
turn, salute in true Court School style, and leave me
in the tent.

They are gone,
and I open my oystered hand to gaze at thy face, and
my tired eyes moisten,
while my heart melts in golden pain.

CONTENTS

OSTIA ANTICA 20
Piety Makes the Roughest Road Smooth   21
The City Life   23
The Augustales   26
One Can't Have Gods Enough   28
We are Half Cousin to the Fish   30
I am Blackberries   31
I Just Work Here   32
Museum   34
The Park and the Snake   36
The Perceptions of a Vanishing World   37
The Message of the Stones   38
'The Third Remove from Reality'   39

LOVE AS IF IT NEVER WAS 41
The Day I Saw Love Die   42
Now, The Trembling Heart   44
On Two Lives   46
A Song Unsung   47
Epiphany in Collapse   48
She Moves Beneath   49
I Would Slip Into You   50

FOR JULIE 53

In All These Years   54
Hand in Hand   58
Countless Poets -A Poem A piece   59
Confetti   60

THE CELLULOID **65**
SERPENT COILS
The Tribe Film   66
She Turns Like a Cow   68
Film [Fragment]   70
Lady   71

TO TEACH IS TO **73**
LEARN, TO LEARN IS
TO TEACH
The Dimming Light   74
Consigned to Hell   79
Visiting Kent Street Summer Carnival   81
Running Down the Years   83

NATURE **88**
TRAMELLED AND
UNTRAMELLED! NATURE
Tripping Through the Triangle   89
The Changing Backyard   92
Fanning Ferns   94
Gardens   97
Williams Sculpted Sanctuary Both   98
Aboriginal and European?

What is a Bichon Frise?   99
Litany of Dogs   101
No Swallows Sweep   104
A Flight of Swallows   105

MOVING THROUGH 107
SPACE AND TIME
The Bosphorus is Burning   108
Below the Apartments, a Park   111
Soho Sojourn   112

DESERT DYING 114
Opening coda   115
Medley of heat water and wind   116
Accelerato and explosive sound shifts   117
The camel's endless plodding   118
Silence extended   119
Low key of endless plodding   120
The changing sacred ochre trade   121
Romance and playful love   122
Ominous death and final sadness   123
Sacred music plays against the sighing   124
of desert wind
Final awareness   125
Traffic and arabic music   126

TOWARDS SONG AND 128
PERFORMANCE
Have You Ever Take a Stone?   129

We Are Each Other's Voyeur 131
One Reads of Songs 133
Liza, Liza 135
River of Dreams 137
Let's Get Going Now 139
Composition Upon Composition 140
Eye to Eye 144

THE SEA IS NOT SMALL IN LOVE 146

A CACAPHONY OF POETS 164
Over the Slabs of Meat 165
Mixing it at Matt's 166
A Coruscating Corona 169
"I Thought You'd Brought Some More Poems" 171
A Sad Café 172
Jazz Piano in a Fernleafed Nightclub 173
Where I'm From 174

MARINA 176
Part 1 177
Part 2 182
Part 3 187
Part 4 195

CHARACTER STUDY 204
Flowers 205
Connections 207

Vision of Dreamtime   209

SHIFTING MOODS **212**
Total Self Concern   213
Soren Kierkegaard   214
Floating Fragments on my 23rd Birthday   215
Indian Summer   216
The Refugees   217

WORDS **221**
THIS WAY AND
THAT
Above the Cluttered Hoses   222
Free Fall   224
A Fragment Towards Kella!   226
Journal de Jour - January 1   227
Trace, Track, Route, Root   229
Towards 'The Ides of March'   230

ELEGY   **234**
I Would Not Have You Otherwise   235

Ostia Antica

Piety Makes the Roughest Road Smooth
Augustine of Hippo

In sight of Rome's seven hills, in the shade of the walls,
He stopped there, dropping his scrip and staff,
Kicking off his sandals, spreading out his cloak
And slipped into pleasant and eternal sleep.

In the mountains, behind the orchard walls
He had listened once again to the tall tale, the long tale
Of the huge domes of Rome, the sweeping Colosseum,
The triumphal arches of the Caesars
And like villagers everywhere
He hitched a ride on the oxen carts
To those silvered streets of Rome.

Rome was an eternal fount of baths,
With mosaics whose heroic stance was that of youths swimming
And forums where the golden tongued orators argued
the very price of corn into flowering ears,
Arming the expeditions against the rhino-plated Africs,
And watched the oxen before their Mithraic death.

[...]

Oh for a small apartment there
Not far from the Thermopolium and an evening drink,
With the Tiber a pleasant morning walk,
And just outside the wall the polis of the dead.
Or perhaps an evening of antic in the theatre,
Or the sweat of straining one's body in the gym.
All of this enough, and more than enough.

The City Life

    An old cock with a lolling head,
I am too crushed on my foul perch
To clarion down dawn for Ostia
Morning city of Rome.

    Only the gay bantam of delusion
Could strut possibility into such streets
Packed tighter than a pomegranate's seeds
And as tasteless as its chewed pips.

    Pallid on this pallet,
With mange in its furs, fleas in its straw,
Even viewing the courtyard raises an itch,
For three goats ram each other,
Kids make a mess on a mound of rubbish,
And the chickens foul the last
Dying branch of shade.
Even the bees have flown
Overswarmed by flies.

                                             [...]

PETER JEFFERY OAM

    I shove past this
And shop at the Thermopolium
Where fine fruit eternally fresh
Hangs pendulous in paint
Above the totting wives
And rotting melons.

    I seek retreat in drink
At Augusto's, finding only
North Afric bilge on tap
The bloody ballast of galleys.

    Too hot with such aridity,
In the baths I soak tepidity,
Amongst the chattering queers with withered stumps,
And all touched up.

    Or if not dead before dusk,
The theatre with a farce in force;
Where door is changed for door,
Wife for wife, whore for whore,
And the crowd's foolish roar
For my discerning snore.

[...]

A GENERAL MUCH TIRED OF WAR

   Or if I break free in a midnight run
Along the solitary moonlit shore,
Hoping to kick high spray and sand,
My sandals only scuff fish heads,
And among the rocks
My toes stub on the shard of pots.

The Augustales

As with the sheeptowns of Yorkshire,
Where, newly come to wealth,
The peasant shepherds thrust up cathedral spires,
Gracing their endless dream - while watching sheep -
Of the ascensional Christ
Bursting in sun from clouds

> This then, no less noble,
> A Court of the Augustales,
> Narcissus mirror for imperial self regard,
> Where in never ending sanction
> Ululation flowed over the new laid bones
> In hymns to political manoeuvres
> Or spectacular alpine rallies,
> While the busts, neon-bright in marble flashed
> above the torches of the priests of progress,
> Who, lustrations done,
> Fell heavy as Hannibal's elephants
> Into a mire of corpulent ease.

[...]

A GENERAL MUCH TIRED OF WAR

No more bright than Belvedere,
With its Monroe mist swirling over the drive-ins,
Or a Valentino purple in vitreous rock
Above a green scunged and scalloped pool,
Or 'art nouveau' stairs ambling amongst antique nudes
Coyly shoving in clitoris with indulgent modesty,
Or the Babe Ruth bat encased in gold,
Spiked as lethal in legend as any Brooklyn slugger.

    Or was this Hall of Fame more subtle?
    Did bourgeois stridency beneath the ascetic sun,
    Let Nature carve its irregular verdict
    Across the etched names on buckled plinths;
    This collapsed line of great men?

One Can't Have Gods Enough

The monumental public gods
Accuse the city with their high indifferent stare,
Accept the ostentation of public recompense
Paid by politicos and prostitute alike.
Recording, in the finery of their drapery,
Histories of cults and guilds and dull official speeches
Masking minor disturbance in most citizens' lives.

The Greek sculptor chiseled their stone into filigree on
his lungs.
And the Afric slave broke his back beneath their marble
blocks.

Such gods humble us in the streets,
But do not see the tupping of maids beneath the stairs,
The glutting of food and drink,
The cut and thrust of the marital bed.
And as incest is most private and horrendous,
So we make our household gods from squat river mud

[...]

Obese, lopsided, smile smirched into leer,
Eccentric and unique as us,
No, we cannot have gods enough.

The Venus aphrodisiac, throbbing out your sex, belly and pudenda distended;
As the serpents twine your legs, make my loving good tonight.
The Mithras bull bellowing against the wall;
Save me from killing him and I'll bathe you in blood.

The Atlas straining against the world;
A bathe of suppliant oil if the rheumatism goes.
Let the moneybags thump like fulsome testes,

For a gold bangle, a shatter of silver flowers.
Ill leave you Turn your eyes as I steal the sweets,
Ill leave you

Inconsequence, sequence, essence
No, we cannot have gods enough.

We are Half Cousin to the Fish

On the Lido, small black Romans eat fruits of the sea,
Spiked anemone, mussel eye and whorled sea snail.
Still dripping salt water as held between the fingers,
They are gulped down as a groper -
Blind with huge dull eyes, mumbles weed on rocks -
Till sated, they belch and flop away
In a dribble of towels and flapping thongs.

But in Ostia the small brown Romans
Dived deep into the element,
With the alertness of a gull sighting flake of fish.
Water held as their port in the hands of the sea,
Thus cradled and rocked, they watched
The sad dying of dolphins in nets,
Or the squids cast down on the mosaics.

No wonder they were brothers to the sea,
And saw the huge marriage feast of Neptune
Where nymphs and horses and gods trailed tails,
Sexual, rhythmic and pulsing through water,
Their proudest stance
Was prone or diving down
Into the raptures of the deep,
Where, in bronzed love, these water gods
Laughed ripples of minnows from their mouth.

I am Blackberries

I, arms akimbo, lie
Deep in the blackberries,
A creeper of flesh and sweat
Amongst this fruit of thorns.

Flaccid as dust,
I lie in my body's tomb,
Till a stirring thought
Ripples through the room,
And rising with deceptive life
My mind settles over all
Patinaing it as my domain
But oh, so insubstantial,
It might be washed away in a freshening rain.
Now in late morn,
I am the cool iced coffee
That swirls around my tongue
And slides down the throat's gully
To my scalloped lungs.
I am the blood in my veins,
The roaring in my ears,
The ructions in my throat.

Rilke's final panther lost
In useless endless motion,
But ever rippling in the poet's eye.

I Just Work Here

A cycle wavered along the chariot ruts,
And the guide shouted up the tourists like sheep.
Night was closing over this place of eternal dreams.

He dropped off his bike, leaned it against a wall
And to share the lingering dusk offered me some wine.

Half light, half mist our conversation tenuous
Over the smoke of my proffered cigarette.

Dim as the wind, our speech fought through the dregs of our tongues
'How many children?' as if fertility was evidence of ultimate virtue.
The place we agreed was 'bella'
but oh so 'anticcha' But life on the Lido was better 'Yes!
and 'Roman clothes are the best!'
And he had a brother 'there in Sydney'
And 'how much did I earn?'
As maestro I became 'a wealthy maestro!'

A GENERAL MUCH TIRED OF WAR

Other guides took the different sites in monthly -
'This week Pompeii, the Nymphs in May,
And in December the Augustales would follow suit.
Oh it was just a job!'

Did the romance of art and the past worry him?
 As thoughts bunch up in frustration -
Heavy as the testes of Hercules -
Guides are turned mad in the end by the Gioconda smile.

No, he was as phlegmatic as pumping tyres.
He mounted up and rode away
Disappearing in the twilight of the Casa de Diana.
The ruins dropped away like a scurry of sheep

Museum

In our unbelieving stare.
We see the midwife tear
A babe from its mother in a chair.
And in the cool vault
Mithras is forever killing the bull,
And broken nosed Pallas
Is still the Chalice of Eternal Beauty -
Strong as stone
Stripped to bone.

Coloured glass beads
Glinting like false opals
Over us like Time's flowering sepals,
Show the Roman past -
A civilisation's death
For our taffeta minds -
In this most tasteful arena,

[...]

A GENERAL MUCH TIRED OF WAR

As tasteful as that day
When above courtiers in wanton play,
Nero unleashed tons of flowers
Drowning their screams in bowers
Of fragrant overscented death.

The Park and the Snake

In the park where a rescued Diana
Protested her innocence two thousand years too late,
To tourists bloated with pleasant wine.
It was no wonder
Beneath the baby's small sarcophagus,
The black snake
Slipped away silent in the leaves

Nature nurtures death on a forgiving breast.
The snake could wait -
Death would coil again from its cast off skin.

Eternal Life is generous to its potential young.

Perceptions of the Vanishing World

In a flash of perception,
Butterflies
Rise from crumpled leaves.
Dew
Covers the ground,
But he sees the single tear
On the rose's withered cheek.

Commonality of phrase,
In speech,
Such caught jewels
Are cast
And scattered.

Jealous,
Of all such
Tourist phrases,
The poet
Watches himself
And holds his tongue.

Until he sets it down
In a book
Rigid casting of print
So that the jewel cannot shift
For yet, a thousand years!
And yet again.

The Message of the Stones

We lie in the pleasant ruin
Of wine and chicken and pizza,
Behind the wall
Away from the wind,
While our wives and children explore
These ruins.

We, however, explore
The two great lands
Italia and Australia.

You see the dry reality
Of sand and heat and flies
Unspoilt by human mounds,
The verities of blood
In the kangaroo brought down in its leap,
Blood oozing from its flesh heap,
And yourself howling atavistic.

And I too far lost in that land
Eyes almost blinded with that sand
Want, in turn, to push up the Tiber
To the spoils of Antica,
Like a tribe of marauders.
Forever setting up wars on maps
Conquering vegetation, wild animals,
And raising cities in their wake.

'The Third Remove from Reality' Plato

In the street the sole weed curls and dies,
The only natural things that stir are flies.

Tufted with marble leaves,
Columns are stone forests beside stone streams
And nature is held only in the paint
Limned on walls enclosing space:
Third remove from the vaporous reality of air.

Though mayhem goes on its wild hunt,
Its spears shattering myriad as blades of grass,
Teeth fanged above slavering jaws,
Horses reared in precise confusion
With flanks flaring above thunderclouds of trampling flesh,
The drowsy bachelors sprawl and drawl
Beneath this pastoral pastel on the wall.

Holding aside a curtain of paint,
A cupid parts some reeds.
I see a duck that swims and one that ducks
Into the submarine world of root and worm,
Above a marital bed
Where tired spouses toss in sheets,
Making travesty of lovers in the grass.
Like the final dream,
Comes this permanent loss of green.

LOVE, As if it Never Was

The Day I Saw Love Die

This day I saw love die.
I saw fear walk across your brow
And trample love underfoot.
I heard your voice like a hollow echoing
From a plaster mask,
And as I watched the swallows of our love
Dart through the window.
A dead smoke of char and ash chilled me.

[...]

A GENERAL MUCH TIRED OF WAR

I left, but I watched the room for a long time,
To see if the golden flame of your hair
Would relight the rain-soaked day,
But you did not come;
I saw the shut window on a dead office ---
The tomb of our love ---
And I thought our love is as if it never was,
As if it were a wisping cloud in a clear sky
And my heart was all in sadness,
I will walk,
   I will walk;
But - alone
Past your fear gutted corpse, unseeing,
For my eyes will be filled with the vision of you,
Of the clear free sun in your hair,
And the soft, peaceful hollows,
And the flowering love that we once so carefully shared;
And I shall be free, and you a slave.

Perenjori, 1957

Now, The Trembling Heart

There was a young prince wandered the towns,
Heroic in his solitude, for upborne he was
By a sustaining love that dwelt native in his mind.
In the peace of empty streets and forlorn bunting,
He remembered a hot sun,
And the sea, and her as free as foam.
It was an emblem engraved in his smiling lips,
His loneliness was fantasia,
Making even the saddest streets populous.

Came the spring,
The crowded carts with sustaining produce,
The laughing couples, the singing wine, and sudden pain.
He was trembling with a flower in his hand,
The petals were damp and perfume,
And he brooded the river, each shape falling like tears.
And as he turned,
From the rail that witnessed his hunger,
He saw another such as she.

[...]

A GENERAL MUCH TIRED OF WAR

They talked awhile, they walked awhile,
The Thames was evening fire,
And their words burst patterning in the air.
The long lone street was full of light,
Sweet rue made sad songs to their feet,
Elegance, like a stately minuet,
walked their hauntling sorrow.
And yet as they did part,
Each lost into themselves - two lonely halls -
And yet, there was a joy in the other's company,
composed of quiet regret.

**Shelbourne Secondary School,
London 1958**

On Two Lives

In the silent whirlpool of raging emotions,
In the secret depths of Life's oceans
There swirls star shot weed
That, clinging to the fate encrusted hulks of other lives,
Forever leaves part of itself tangled in the vessel's screw.

So, it was with you and me -
Save for the rust red of my blistering kiss
Your sides were virgin white,
And my weed choked heart
had a swathe of softness cut across it.
 Our footsteps mingled partly in the sand,
And like those of two frightened gulls
left off in unfulfilment.

My sweet, does another dolphin roam your watery halls?
Or does my ghost echo down the caverns of your heart
And your eyes sequin with hope from a distant sun?
And your heart's sight recede a haze in the desert waste?

Perth, 1956

A Song Unsung

She sits in a dappled room,
Weaving her cloth of symbols with the ribbon of Life;
Her heart is a pearl cased tomb.

She was a song unsung,
Her thighs unsounded melody,
Her teeth white bells unrung.

Her lips mouthed the song,
A timbre of tune wined his head, but no sound,
No lark's poem, no trembling gong.

And his crystal heart tumbled
Into a thousand sunlights under the baton of Life,
And the delicate thread of song forever fumbled.

He cries in a sunwhite street,
His torn throat bleeding, singing silent sorrow,
And the thorns of love tear his feet.

Perth, June 1954
Published in CENTAUR 30 / 6 / 1954 Published in PELICAN, 1957

Epiphany in Collapse

Lost as he is in the melancholy of betrayed love,
He scuffs desultory through the endless sand,
Then lifts his head to the de Chirico metaphysic
Of shore, sea and sky - alternating horizons.

Glancing down, his feet awash in the incoming tide,
he sees a dead gull blown
in the swirl of the advancing surge,
wings outspread in beatific glory
of ever in-breathing freedom.

His eyes rise and dance along the horizon.
Heartened by the ever incoming, ever restoring breeze,

He feels the pull of the retreating water.
But suddenly looking down at his feet he sees
A mere flurry of discordant feather and deserted bone,
A charnel pile that mirrors his despairing love.

Generated in a Lucy Dougan workshop 2018

She Moves Beneath

She beneath my hand with grace,
She rears, holds, falls away with breathless pace.
White arrow thrust of desire,
Head flamed in fire, How can she be held?
When she yields
Her richness snows my hand's field,
And the only thing that remains
Is the sheet's yellowing stains.

Yunderup,
Easter Sunday 1974

I Would Slip Into You

I would slip into you
Quicker than knife into butter.
Time would fade faster than snow
And from where I lay
The ceiling would be the same.

A sigh would drift from your belly and thighs
Through your lips, from your eyes,
And we would stroke each other's flanks Absent mind-
edly.

Outside the window the rosemary would blow.

FOR JULIE

Many wives poets feel that they should have a poem a day dedicated to them as if they were the Muse

And so it was with Julie even though I kept cautioning her with the old maxim 'Vanity! Vanity! Saith the Lord'

So to protect myself and her from any misadventure I have enlisted the devices of Cento and another device named Confetti which enlist first lines etc. from the poetic universe, even to the point of enlisting the Vincent Writing Centre Group I co-ordinate , so both Muse and wife are well served served by blaming the besotting of we poets to the muse in the work of our fellows.

In All These Years
On our wedding day, Sunday 25 September 2005

In all these years
You have never written me a poem!
Now Julie -
Along with Gough
I feel it's time, it's time!
Now's the time!

Twenty four years
Waiting for this... Good boy! Good boy! Y
ou deserve a kiss.

'Do you love me?'
You ask me sweetly every day.

'Waddaya reckon?' I say.
'Of course I do!
In each and every way!
I love you, oh, for so many things.

[...]

A GENERAL MUCH TIRED OF WAR

From that first day, Our tentative foray
You treat me to a Chinese meal -
To make us equal, you pay.

In turn, I treat you
To a weekend hotel in Armadale.
On the tv, the 'Rose Bowl'
Players clad in rainbow, their bodies thudding!

In light all-streaming
My finest drawing is of you in the hotel bed.
Our bodies hugging,
A happiness in our nakedness.

The nakedness of our children,
The first almost strangled by cord at birth,
And oh, how you curse,
Until you cry into laughter and thanks,
Her little lips at your breast.

After long discussions and with mutual consent,
Our second sleek rabbit stretches at his full length,
A glowing nakedness, in his total elegance.

[...]

Naked have we all come,
And naked shall we go -
Past property, social due, and abrupt angers,
Past youthful beauty, pain and powerful strength -
To the raw and naked simplicity
Of each trying to be true to each
Modulating and enjoying our complicity.

In mutual laughter, our life is at its best.
Our good humour crushes the rough into smooth,
And we laugh at and with the world.
Our strident and raucous joy
 Settles into the calmness of a grin,
And broadens into a smile
That is joyous in its sharing with our friends.
Or then alone, together,
The great silver screen flickering
Above our heads and dancing eyes,
Transports us together into the shining
Of our strange and beautiful world.

[...]

A GENERAL MUCH TIRED OF WAR

So many memories linger,
Like scattered shells still for us to finger -
Venice and ourselves as Empress and Emperor
As we swirl into the Grand Canal.
Or Moreno in the alps,
Where we watch the torrent
Slashing its central highway of foam,
Past spa, casino, opera house and avenues of pine.

Or old Prague, medieval,
Or Bratislava, fairytale Palace from story book

Or, and sweetest and simplest of all,
The old bed in the Albergo di Sole,
That sloped us inwards and downwards
Into an erotic tangle,
That resumed our lives and a mutual history.

   When we wake, you often say
   'Remember to be kind to Julie!'
Oh Julie, Julie!
And now we are 'we'
Let's hold hands and come to bed!

Hand In Hand

She whispers, "A pianist's hand",
But it has never played across the keys.
Lies there a smooth waste
That can only be filled by her own -
Quietly yearning for contact, but comforting me?

Now so many years on,
The concealing of the top of the hand Is a cover of veins and lines,
Melanoma bright here and random lines there
Old as my eighty years and more
Nostalgia bright, but oh so bright beginning,
That has lasted through all our years.

WAPI Perth Poetry Festival Workshop
12 August 2016

Countless Poets— A Poem A Piece

10.	I gaze up at the sky and wonder
13.	Have I loved in vain
22.	Such beauty unheard of
59.	I thought I would give up my life
52.	If we never met
61.	Because my feelings
43.	As the human heart is fickle
71.	I should have gone to sleep
84.	With a lonely heart
25.	Are you paying for even a moment
99.	There's no escape in this mad world
93.	Like water rushing down
113.	Though I am not good enough
115.	Pining for you
107.	How I would like to show you
90.	I believed in you with all my heart
101.	I spent the night in longing
29.	Thoughts of a thousand things
57.	Blown by the fierce winds
67.	As I will soon be gone
19.	My heart is tangled
20.	For you
25.	For even a moment
64.	Will you promise you'll never forget

Rita La Bianchi
Vincent Writing Group.

Confetti

Camerado, I give you my hand !
I give you my love more precious than money,
I give you myself before preaching or law;
Will you give me yourself?
Will you come travel with me?
Shall we stick by each other as long as we live?
Walt Whitman from 'Song of the Open Road'.

Why do I love? Go, ask the glorious sun
Why every day it round the world doth run.
'Ephelia'

And the sunlight clasps the earth,
    And the moonbeams kiss the sea!
What is all this sweet work worth
    If thou kiss not me ?
Percy Bysshe Shelley

[...]

Drink to me only with thine eyes,
    And I will pledge with mine;
Or leave a kiss in the cup,
    And I'll not look for wine.
Ben Jonson

' Love me, for I love you' - and answer me
' Love me, for I love you' - so we shall stand As happy
equals in the flowering land
Of love, that knows not a dividing sea.
Christina Rosetti

To have you without stint and all I can
Today, tomorrow, world without an end.
Christina Rosetti

How blessed I am in discovering thee!
To enter into these bonds, is to be free;
Then where my hand is set, my seal shall be.
John Donne

[...]

I would I could adopt your will,
See with your eyes, and set my heart
Beating by yours , and drink my fill
At your soul's springs, - your part my part
In life, for good and ill.
Robert Browning

Thou, O my soul, my flesh, and my blood!
Then come the wild weather, come sleet or come snow,
We will stand by each other, however it blow.
Henry Wadsworth Longfellow

Mankind should hope, in wedlock's state,
A friend to find as well as mate.
Mary Savage

What is it men in women do require?
The lineaments of Gratified Desire.
What is it women do in men require?
The lineaments of Gratified Desire.
William Blake

Happy be the bridegroom,
And happy be the bride:
And may not man, nor bird, nor beast
This happy pair divide
Anonymous

[...]

Again the feast, the speech, the glee,
The shade of passing thought, the wealth
Of words and wit, the double health,
The crowning cup, the three - times - three.
Alfred, Lord Tennyson

The bloated wassailers will never heed -
Let us away, my love, with happy speed.
John Keats

Oh Christ! That I were in my bed
And you lying by my side.
Folk saying.

When a man has married a wife, he finds out whether
Her knees and elbows are only glued together.
William Blake

True love is a durable fire,
In the mind ever burning,
Never sick, never old, never dead,
From itself never turning.
Sir Walter Raleigh

The Celluloid Serpent Coils

The Tribe Film
For Peter, Barry, Geoff, Ivan, Luba and Rae

Running Water, Floating Cloud
Have become Broken Lance, Torn Arrow,
Their souls streaming farther than faintest star.

We will come together
Not in play or dance or song
But in work.
Can I love you
As delicately as the way
You press the camera's switch,
As constantly as you
Record the shots,
As intently as you
Graph the sound,
As patiently as you
Wheel the dolly,
As brightly as you
flare the lights?

[...]

A GENERAL MUCH TIRED OF WAR

Can I hold you as generously as our dream,
Or will I see you
As minutes on a sheet?
As dollars in a budget -
Dull celluloid in a can?

No, the tribe remembers only the hunt
For the white buffalo's skin,
And not all the shattered ponies,

And the shallow graves of broken men.
Running Water, Floating Cloud
Have become Broken Lance, Torn Arrow,
Their souls streaming farther than faintest star.

Fremantle Arts Centre Press
SOUNDINGS
1976

She Turns Like a Cow

She turns like a cow!

She flounces and bounces,
Like
a
blood
- ee
cow.

Action!

Dah-ling
Lift that leg
Ever so genteelly

Cut! No!
She flounces
like the cow
she is.

[...]

Lover-ly
But not what
We want.

Lover!
Lift your foot so
you don't
crush the snail.

Lover-ly!
Just like the lady
We know you are.

It's a wrap!

And now the silver screens
Hold a common Brooklyn girl
More decorous
Than Cleopatra descending
Temple steps.

Film Fragment

From the serpent's egg the world writhes.
And the celluloid fragment shifts.
It rears away
From its spiralling purpose;
Its lignum subsides back into the yoni.

With events more mysterious than Melies -
Master that he was -
The Lumieres show a train dragon Belching fire and
smoke;
A factory crowd grimly setting out for home;
And in a Church a shadow faltering falls
Over a cast of Christ,
While in a kitchen a child breaks and eats bread.

And to make universal laughter,
As a gardener moves his hose from bed and bed,
A hidden urchin doubles it behind him,
And with its cessation of water
And sudden spluttering, squirting release
Turns it into a veritable giocchi d'acqua,
Drenching the face of the puzzled gardener.

Lady

Lady
Such warm lips
Such bright eyes
And I
Abashed
Come
Come again
People about
Glasses curled round fingers
Rose
White
Red
Anxious
I
Perplexed
Lost you
Come
Come again
Warm
Voice and my sigh
Lost in smoke
See you
South
See you
Again
Soon

To Teach is to Learn, To Learn is to Teach

The Dimming Light

She could so easily have been the pantomime boy,
and flattened down for Peter Pan,
or would it be Puck
with her sharp alert eyes and page-boy or even monkish cut,
and that abrupt stab of cigarette, held so languidly the moment before.
But what need had she of that,
for with her extended arm and flick of palm,
she had a total and directional will
that could conjure up Cleopatras, Joans,
Lady Bracknells, Lysistratas,
and what you will to please us all,
even as her body held its own sense of theatre.

So that some of us would rather watch her behind
the scenes or in the director's seat
than anyone she drew across the stage.

[...]

A GENERAL MUCH TIRED OF WAR

Brown as a berry and hard as a nut,
she was sharp bramble and delicate rose and rich fruit
and everywhere.

She regarded the world with her skeptic's eye
Skipping, dancing, darting
In mock disbelief and suspended optimism,
But with her gentle deprecation yet generous regard
she hardened us for disappointments that might come,
yet softened us in humour with each and every success,

trimming our ambition to a proper sense of itself,
allowing us to be light with most serious purpose.

I remember her like a taskmaster as she sweated on the
Murdoch arena,
open to the pines and the skies,
levying the student slaves on their Egyptian pyramid,
pointing out this and that,
yet no sooner said than done.
For she refused to wait
for what must rightly come
even bringing on the Midnight of the New Year
with a delighting and self-indulgent imperious rush.

[...]

She ran the canon of drama
and lashed any student who neglected a period,
determining to show that each age
had its own logic of theatre,
and the absence of this knowledge was truly
vulgar and boorish.

In theatre she disdained flatulent talk
of what might be, should be, could be
for she always knew what would be!

Her intellect was in her action
Shrewd moves of thought were strokes of paint on the flat,
the tuck of the costume, the flash of the head, the pointed toe,
and relentlessly and ever rehearsing with the repeated but varied speech
and she even hafted the head onto the spearman's staff.

[...]

A GENERAL MUCH TIRED OF WAR

And my next to last memory
Was of us on a sandy beach
Climbing a twisting erstwhile hilly path
To search for her house nearby or hereabouts
To find her at the head of her haven
Staring down as if our visit was as regular or common-
place from the tradesman
Rather than our three-year absence and friendship's
drought.

And by her a small dog ran
But mistily I saw a sheepdog, well out of its clime
big as a moving haystack, grinning foolishly
and as medieval as Chaucer,
bumping against her, tangling its rope
and trying to tumble her feet,
and by her side a gruff but loving man
who delightfully drowned me with gin
as we gazed down some passing sunset as colonial and
imperial as India -
'Hot curry and pukka, sahib' and 'What say you sir?'
and she moved us past the flying angel in the garden
into her house for a slice of cake and a cup of tea.

So many friends, so many Noelanns,
So many gifts, so many thanks,
Each of us has a poem for her,
An essay of love in its truest sense,
And she will justly mark them all,

But secretly be pleased
That her work is a footnote for all our lives

In Rome they said that when she went
a breath had gone from the world
making it the lesser for it,
but is she that spritish Bremer breeze
the Southern doctor of our late afternoon
of memorising and nostalgic love

As, in pale imitation,
we watch the sunset from her seat
with our paperback, our cigarette and
our cold glass of wine.

Consigned to Hell
The Academic Board meets and consigns a student to hell.

The square conclave
Forced by our 70 into a gravity,
That the pioneering 10 women never dreamed
Though their fluttering vanity
Played at the game of ceremony,
Meditates
On the faults of Stan Sod off
Who never prepared his lesson notes
[all lecturers turn up your notes, please]
who thumped a kid with a good back-hander
[what father has never used the flat of his hand in the right place?]
spoke indistinctly
[embarrassing interview wasn't it with his voice choked down?]
came in drunk and disorderly

[...]

[that's why all the staff functions are held on Friday nights]
and tried to make love to the head mistress
[It would be beyond you all to deal with them all] then negotiates.

'He's a rat, but not as bad as Jones.'
'He at least had his name on the cover.'
'The boy at least got up,'
'Who wouldn't make a pass?'
Pontificates
'He would be a blot on the teaching profession and
'certificate.'
'Let's get rid of him and send him out to school.
He just might learn something!'

Sunderland,

Visiting Kent Street Summer Carnival

Carnival is a jewel box
set in a land of hotels, schools, cafes
and even a brothel.
Its necklace spells out, the length of Kent Street
and the sound of drumming fills the air,
a touch of Africa and then a circle of all of us
drumming a response to the lead,
and then the market a cornucopia of food
of fruit and vegetables, sweets, exotic ethnic meals and
demonstrations of yoga and Thai dancing
and children making art of their own swirling
in foot races and around an adult leader,
and here in the Arts Centre
leaves fall from the trees and pattern textiles,
Stanley knives cut into soft lino but make
Feathering lines of delicate plants.
A water colourist moves her paint as thickly as oils,
has a confining line that like Chinese brush
etches out the elegance of two sensual models,

[...]

a slide machine ricochets landscapes, architecture, and
portrait,
ceramicists plunge their hands in clay and bring up long
vases of beauty,
and all along are passages of tiles.

And here
we sit out the front scribbling flickers of thought
to bring all of the carnival into words on paper,
a record of all this creativity, exuberance, and joy,

True ending of this April season of arts
And all for this year!

So what of the next?

Running Down the Years
[Modern School Reunion, 1985]

O sodales ...
No!
Moderna scola, nostra scola
Semper gloriam ...
No!
Moderna scola, scola alma
O sodales concinamus,
Nostra scola, te amumus
Simper gloriam petamus.

Fading memory of that foreign tongue
Bats words across time's wire fence
As we did hand tennis balls
To fill out our long sunglazed recess.

[...]

Made scholars by contest
And public in newspapers -
From Bridgetown, Dalkeith, North Perth,
From city, suburb, and country town -
Through five studied years
We were marked to be marked
In this most public of public schools,
To move through hope and confusion,
From child, pupil to person.

Our teachers moved us
With humour, tact, satire, praise
And occasional care and kindness
Through columns, grammars, experiments,
Through planes, diagrams, elements
As one said
'To crank the handle'
For our future success.

Even to draw -
Freedom of space and line -
We never moved beyond
The school tower or porch,
Our lino-cut and graphite
Constrained by the marks
Of final and stated result.

[...]

Yet those teachers
Marked by rumour or public
Saturdays Hinted at wider freedoms
Of blazing wickets and thunderous goals,
Waited and charted our Inland Sea
Or watched rock quiet
On a headland of occupied Timor,
And celebrated with us in sport.

So we are running down the years,
Past minor rebellion,
Where we are larrikin and innocent as Anzac,
We burned blank cartridge cordite for stumpy rockets
That scored the Sphinx memorial,

Made forays into the shops of town,
Played 'Boogie Woogie' at a Chopin Concert.
To call out the Head, sentinel in stony silence to his study door,
Smoked strong Dutch tobacco in the thinnest paper,
Became baseball bandits and rugby rebels
And continually made round rulers square.

[...]

We are running down the years,
Freemasons in sport,
In circles of white,
Scoring goals from kick-off,
Premierships from three under
And the cry of 'Up and under!'
To make us six in front.
Past the girls in blue,
Florid in swirls of white,
Last of the romantics
In love with our own earnestness
And flurried by life.

We are running down the years
To a clear and green and golden dusk,
Where past all desire,
To leap and pace, to vault and kick,
To mark and strike, to arch and dive.
Past all the impediment
Of linament and straps and bandages
Of spikes and studs and plates.
We are running down the years
Past falter, lurch and slide,
To reach that even stride, effortless glide
 that half laps all the others,
in less than that day's final mile.

Nature Tramelled And Untramelled!

Tripping Through the Triangle

As if they were astronomers, the other keen-eyed ones
saw the myriad of flowers
In the densest space of not more than two boot lengths
square
As if they were brightest stars to name
But all I saw was a plethora of weeds.

And so it was to my untutored eye my ear for names saw/
heard
And who knows
I may have taken up the long learning and seeing of flora
- fauna - bund,
That fills the others with a similar control that has made
them the lord and ladies of the universe.

[...]

Prickly Moses and by Jesus all I saw was a wisp with the faintest fan
And even then had I seen what he had thought I should
And how many others would happily blaspheme
This and that, that and this,
Erecting biblical temples for companionate walking.

Much better then his tale of Nuyts Floribunda and its Christmas tree flowering,
That even blind Freddy couldn't disregard and the Dutch so easily name
As they named the Rats Nest that has become a paradise for school leaving and loving couples.

And then came the paperbarks with their peeling layers of skin
As long and as short and as prolific as the long string of sunburn peelings
That, in the dusk, whiled away the blazing sun
Of head and body resting on towel and sand.

Even more powerful for me when my indigenous friend pointed out the paperbarks by the river
and bursting into tears said,
'I was borned under that tree!'
And I thought of 'the troubles he had seen!'

[...]

A GENERAL MUCH TIRED OF WAR

And then an arboreal Belsen of dieback or Bush fire
scarred trunks
In a massacre triangle of their own,
A writhing twisted parody of the normal tangle of the
upright green saplings
That once they had been

Was it ever thus, the saplings pushing thrusting against
each other,
Or as we left in the fading sun
did they lie together in sweet exhaustion?
Mount Lawley
27 August 2020

The Changing Backyard

The lemon lime freshly cut,
the dying lavender finger rolled
Leaving the lingering scent of childhood prospects,
That Mediterranean rush of fig, olive, loquat, mulberry,
lemon, cumquat
and even pomegranate,
Planted in gardens and all around us
By those hard workers and the newly arrived
In productive, fruitful abundance and nostalgia
For their earlier constant labouring rural life.

But from my backyard step I saw none of this,
Only the newly lawn-mowered Kikuyu grass
In and around the metallic tree of the Hills hoist.

[....]

Now this view was two shades
above the green grass of painted concrete,
of what eventually came to replace
the earlier plethora of fruit,
effacing, obliterating, pointlessly mulching
all that these same people had earlier planted then ne-
glected
for the dancing clusters of fruit fly, richly mouldering,
abandoned or hacked away.

Arthritic now, those early planters
Have moved beyond that hard rural labour
Into a life of somnolent comfort and ease.

Sue Clennell Workshop / 2015

Fanning Ferns

Here in our dry lands, the trees are mostly saplings,
Making screens that spring apart and back, as one intrudes,
Larger than shrubs, but just.
One finally can not see one's companion , and by then
Will have come upon a shaggy barked tree and then another,
A stride away and is comfortably lost.
And so one moves through swathes of whip back sticks
And over bare gravelled rock all small stones and wisps
Of grass, and then, run up to boulders and jutting cliff.

But here in this wetter land, with
The chill around one's shoulders like a sodden scarf,
One can scarcely see the trees so occluded are they
By white green, green white stemmed fans of ferns.
Their stems set one's teeth on edge, all pith and tear apart,
Like sugar drenched cane.

[...]

And one's thoughts are all deep green
Or spreading white, and have a misty epiphany of hidden trunks,
Metal sheened behind the layering ferns,
Like the stripper's seventh veil thrown away,
Part in triumph, part as vapour, revealing
That shining tube of pink white powder drenched flesh.

Once the kauris were thick,
So wherever one turned they were barriers each to each,
Scarcely tolerant of human movement through them,
Searching for a clearing of beyond, where one might strike camp,
Being settlement of mining shafts, rail-track slats carving trails
Of timber, of gold, and allowing the water to seep
In that space of denuded kauri, and lead to gumbooted alluvial dredging
In tightly held and delicately tilted pan, so that when
The gold dried up, the endless fires of kauris
burnt down to ash.
The ferns began their relentless march,
In, around, over, under the ever-dying strangled kauri.

[...]

Like a pile of Venetian masks layered each over each other,
The ferns fan and spread relentlessly
like the Mongol horde in stampede,
obliterating any hint of anything but themselves,
as our little toy train hurtles around and around
spiralling the mountain, everything is trickling damp.

So here and there,
with springing stems and spreading fronds
there is only a camouflage over the stray arrant trees
that speak of an earlier time.

Mount Lawley
Tuesday 21 July 2015

Gardens

Will overgrow
If we die or not

Flowers will boom
With our love or not

Leaves Will drift
To mud and rot.

1973

William's Sculpted Sanctuary Both Aboriginal and European?

I am there with William, or am I?
His living friends are embossed, impressed
Into the index of trunks, boulders,
Waterways, as if sprites abounded,
Had crept up on us in pleasing startled unawareness,
recognisable, as Peter Pan in our Queen's Gardens.
Driven as yet they are with European sensibility,
But they want to sink like Nolan's dying stockman
Into his perish, deeply merging into grass.

Reassuring as a colouring-in book of nursery rhymes.
Almost as twee as Snugglepot and Cuddlepie,
My anxiety then of his and our Pansophist sentiment.

And yet amongst my Indigenous friends
There are tales of Min Min,
Men smaller, tinier than us,
Intermittently juddering between a conceal and reveal,

Elvish, impish, a shade of flickering thought.
They were of a earlier tribe that roamed,
Then fled through the bush, away from massacre
And leaving the trees, scrub and open plain
To those we have come to call the First People,
And now finally us - the Settler Invaders.
Sue Clennell Workshop / 2015

What is a Bichon Frise?

A handful powder puff of white
with a bark bigger than his bite
and a mouthful breath like a suppressed fart
keen to chew the sweat off your finger
but all cuddle and heaving spotty tum

Yoshi fronts any of the Alsatians
provided he stands behind Julie's legs,
and is reluctant to walk the long way to the park
but is like a whippet to get back home.

Forever near the fridge and my treats,
bits fortuitously falling from my fingers.
So sad then when food appealed no more,
his eyes glazing into blindness
and his nose sniffing my heel
or lost in all directions, with nowhere home.

[...]

The final stroking of his life
running through my fingers.
The lift in my chest, the watering in my eyes,
and him slipping softly away,
far from those delicious cuddles
between us in our morning bed.

Oh Yoshi were that you were back with me,
not as a screen on my phone, but
smelly, noisy, naughty, hungry,
spotty tummy and furcloud in my hand.

Litany of Dogs

Cold nippy night
and I almost leave the dogs in the laundry
Rather than walk up to the highway and back,

Old Khandi with her cataracts
and Yoshi with his little legs
a matter of stop and start,
sniffing ponder and rush forward,
and that tell tale circle and stoop
and when suddenly complete
the back upright and in a straight surge forward
Yoshi acts as if nothing has happened.

But we are not alone for every second house has a dog
and I sometimes meet their owners while my dogs growl
at his or her pet and I assure them my dogs
are all bark and don't bite.

[...]

And as dogs resemble people so there's good and bad
in the neighbourhood as one progresses up the street.
The little dog in the Italian house that eyes the street
Through the small crack beneath the door in the wall,
And slides away if one rushes towards him,
His bark caught somewhere at the back of his throat.

Then there is Patch who has yapped endlessly for hours
and rushes back and forth in his front yard
and tells the whole street there is movement afoot.

And then the chill of the two Alsatians
who bustle each other away down the passage
from their kitchen and try to hurtle
through the fly wire front door
until they are snappily called back.
Sometimes they are confronted in the street, luckily on leash
And Yoshi growls loudly behind my trouser leg
As if he would willingly tear them apart.

Many leave their door open to catch any flurry of air,
so the next house has a smaller dog that mine never meet
But who has already sensed my dog's promenade,
And his recurring yelp is passed with complete disdain.

[...]

Across the street behind walls of different houses,
dogs invisible and hard to count fill the air
with resounding yelp and bark and snarl.
The street is almost full orchestra.

And then the final house with the littlest dog
that if met is sniffed by Yoshi in friendly enquiry
or if too close to Khandi gains a warning yap
or a rolling ruction that threatens thunder.

Highway met, we turn back for home,
And like some sprinter from the blocks Yoshi's kaleido-
scope of ecstatic release
Contradicts his earlier slow saunter and halts,
and within a quarter of time he is in the house
stretched happily dozingly on the rug by the heater.

Mount Lawley / 9 August 2016.

No Swallows Sweep

O my Lord, no swallows sweep my arcless soul,
Through my blood sings no sad choir of song,
My heart is unstaked, unmartyred; no arrows fly!

My pride is a bloody flag that no wind stirs,
I march in the loneliness where no crowds cheer,
I fall in tar stained sand where no flame burns.

I am lost, O Lord, no stars do guide!
I am naked, O Lord, no garments sheathe my skin.
Succour me, O Lord.
Let swallows sweep.

Perth

A Flight of Swallows

Drifting slow traceries of flight,
The swallows dart through the darkening stand,
As it drips silver in the waning sun,
And the green spears of grass struggle upwards
Against the moistened wood.

We watch from the car,
And see the sad peace of a fading day
Walk through the streets;
Hear the clang of kitchens,
The praying of grace,
And the rustle of evening papers.

Still the swallows come;
Little brushstrokes on the sky's marbled paper,
They slash upwards, then downwards, then away,
Like random thoughts that fleck the brain.

Perenjori

Moving Through Space and Time

The Bosphorus Is Burning
For Orhan Pamuk

Istanbul is flightscape and night scape
As we drift into the airport with its long straggling emigration queue,
Then unquestionably swift with its custom check
That left all to 'Inshallah' and contraband notwithstanding.

Unlike old Hong Kong with its planes zooming down
And up past the skyscrapers, the airport is miles from the city,
And we hurtle up the freeway in total darkness in our minibus
Running everlong along the Bosphorus,
But it is ever disappointingly blank with its blackness and suspect waters,
While on the landside, old fortress walls, nightclubs and waterside cafés.
Are abrupt splashes of light amongst the ever-present darkness.

[...]

Just once or twice like small shimmering chains
We see the lights of vessels moving endlessly with commerce and tide
But they are phantomlike, glowworm-length trails of light,
Minor phosphorence and a mere hint of the great
Bosphorus burning in daylight.
Yet you tell us of a small boy in a cold autumn dawn -
Awake long before the sleeping aunts and uncles
In the slowly decaying family mansion -
With his flickering torch learning a compulsory mantra
for school and his scarcely ageing nation
   'O flag, o glorious flag
    Waving in the sky!'
Gazing into the fading darkness of the Bosphorus.

And sudden the sky all lit up in a thunderclap of sound,
As two tankers ramslammed into the other,
Trailing long paths of flames that made water boil, And like a coruscating necklace
Fired petrol depots one after the other along the shore.

                                                        [...]

The next morning from our postage stamp hotel I heard
the muezzins call
And drawing the curtains I too saw the Bosphorus
A flame in shimmering light, with the endless chain
Of steamers, ferries, launches, warships, yachts
Speeding and wallowing and skimming and chugging
Towards Asia and Europe, Europe and Asia
Endlessly burning the Bosphorus in light and life.

Below the Apartments, A Park
For Glenn

There was time and a space
marked out in the park below
the apartments. Old people slapped
down the mahjong chits and raising
their heads triumphantly eyeballed
their fellow players. Young couples
clung to each waltzing other, not
crudely belly-rubbing, but moving
into sinuosity all the same, while dogs
trailed their leads between the moving
feet, avoiding the stumble and failing
body, and barking companionate to
those lucky enough to be in ladies' laps.
while on the edge, little boys ninjaed
and kung fued with willowy sticks, that
swayed in a cooling breeze. later in the
evening the old men held their
caged birds to the waning moon as
the crowd dwindled away.

WAPI Perth Poetry Festival
3 August 2016

Soho Sojourn

Do you remember that time in Soho
When we wandered away from the wives
and we talked to that girl
who said, 'Had we the time and the money?'
and you said, 'Shouldn't we get back to the girls?'
and passed it all off as an amusing diversion,
and be smart saying
'Man is polygamous, woman monogamous.' and we did
didn't we?
Or ...

Did you go back later?

Desert Dying

Inspired by the Afghan camel drivers and their contribution to Australia. This piece was a collaborative performance between

Arthur Gracias, a Master of Jazz fusion & Peter Jeffery OAM *and appeared several times on WTV-44.*

OPENING CODA
[overture which fades into thoughtfulness]

Holding each other's hands, the keeper welcomes,
But his eyes are drinking in the strangeness
Of the long thin line of discarded shoes,
And hot as the sun is on his back,
He hears and feels the coolness of running water
As he laves his hands and feet
And walks up the stairs to see
Two old men, one sleeping and the other staring into space,

MEDLEY OF HEAT WATER AND WIND
[runs lowkey under voice]

He asks after them and is told
That they are lost in a forty-year limbo
For no one survives them in Afghanistan,
The sounds of their village are whisper on the wind,
Mere ripples of memory.
And they are here to watch the sunset of their days,
A little melancholic, a little sad,
And perhaps stupefied by the intense summer sun

ACCELERATO AND EXPLOSIVE SOUND SHIFTS
As the camel is broken in to the point of its final acceptance of the discipline of bridle and harness the music is lowkey but breaks through with alternate bursts of emphasis and softness.

Sand flies, hands clap clap, slap slap, as the youth dances
and scuffles around the young camel,
which snorts and stamps and sighs in a long chain of
spittle, puffing ever from its mouth
As in its confusion, it scurries, stands, and breaks,
The rope ever doubling, ever shortening in the young
man's hands ever shortening,
Until the camel capitulates in a gentle subsidence,

THE CAMEL'S ENDLESS PLODDING
[an ever-strengthening sense of the camel moving through all kinds of terrain]

As the camel rises, its saddle and bridle bells jingling
the breaker becomes rider and clambers aboard.
Tentative, the camel lurches forward and moves
Its first step of the countless miles
With the sound of scuffling over rocks and the hooves on pavement
And the legs splashing through water
And ever the endless susurrus of the eternal miles
through desert sands.

SILENCE EXTENDED

Absolute stillness here in Australia,
The whirring of stars and a gentle breeze over the flickering fire.
The cameleer stirs and pulls his blankets closer
For warmth and to bury his head
away from the morning sun.

And then he lurches full eyed into wakefulness.
As the cattle low and the camels snort in sympathy
And the bird's morning chorus begins

He rises and pokes the fire, livening it
And stirs the daily rice in the pan. l
Fingers full, he licks the paste until sated.

Then he moves around among the camels
Patting their noses and bodies vigorously
As he yanks down the rope and pulls their heads
Down to the water in sudden splashing
And the long lap lap of drowning thirst.

Until they rise full bellied for the tightening of packs,
And the movement forward in the morning cool,
To the next place of evening rest and calm.

LOW KEY OF ENDLESS PLODDING

Adelaide, the City of Churches - bastion of Christendom
But yet with a solitary mosque which in turn
Was the site of all beginnings across the desert to Perth,
With its second mosque built as a receptacle of faith
And the final destination of the ceaseless wandering
trains of camels.
With the forever camels loading with
the endless tying and untying of ropes

And cities forever fading away in mirage.
Plodding over rock and mud and deep dunes of sand,
Sometimes through the startling sea of blood of Sturt
peas, and past balls of tumbling spinifex.

The upraised waving arms of the lone fringe farmer
In fellow greeting as his flocks traced the thin lines of
edible grass.
And in the isolation of silence and loss of landmark
the echo of the phantom herds of camels and goats.

THE CHANGING SACRED OCHRE TRADE

Earlier than the Silk Route, the ochre tracks criss-cross
Australia, with countless holy quests crossing tribal
boundaries in sacred need.
But now, nestled with the silks, ornaments, iron fittings,
A hundred weight of ochre is carefully moistly packed
Delivering a hundred-fold in one journey
Cutting short endless odysseys in the instant,
And making a bridge with the dark people that few white
people ever achieved.

ROMANCE AND PLAYFUL LOVE

Romances rather than rapes, hennaed hands clasping black,
The giving of gifts and a sort of marriage
Black hair and black eyes shaded,
The play of cloth over her hands
The endless pacing of bangles and bracelet on her arms
The desert wind and her creeping under his blanket.

OMINOUS DEATH AND FINAL SADNESS

The years passing so quickly,
Laughter, lullaby for a child, the mingling with female buyers,
A play between their words and the daily prayers -
The ominous sound of her lingering death-
Perhaps the hacking cough, the croaking song,
The wailing of a male and the echo of his dogs.

The final sitting on the steps and the endless blank stare into space
Reverberates to the sound of the jingling saddle bells
And the harnessing of the camel train.

SACRED MUSIC PLAYS AGAINST THE SIGHING OF DESERT WIND

Lone rider, alone all years but cradled by Allah,
So never alone, while one hears the call of the muezzin,
Speaking with the imam, running through the endless scales of the Koran,
Or, away, solitary in the endless canyons of space
Of desert nights and stars.
Deep dawn and riding into the whistling of the desert wind
And shifting sands that turns into the turbulence of the dust storm,
Then, drowns in the endless quiet that follows in the calm when the wind falls,
And towards dusk a light dances, ever shimmering on the horizon,
And ever with the spreading of the mat and the calling up of prayers,
Until, the cold moon and the hint of soughing palms
Leads one to sleep on the mat in sand to snore softly,
And now in the last years, alone in a doze,
In the dead still of the Perth mosque in late afternoon.

FINAL AWARENESS

To myself now staring deep into their dark eyes,
Kohl rimmed to blunt and shade the blinding light,
Still worn yet no camels to yoke, but this endless habit
Reassures and ensures a small daily oasis,
That will take them to Paradise,
Sans country, sans family, sans camel train, sans memory
Until the single piercing call from the tower
That runs the heights into the Perth blue sky,
Fades to mere running water and the mosque's tranquil quiet,

TRAFFIC AND ARABIC MUSIC

But against the increasing roar of outside traffic
In Perth's growing metropolis,
Is the rustling bustle of a market in Afghanistan,
The yelping call up of the rising camel train
And finally, the soft murmur of the endless Koran.

Perth

Towards Song And Performance

Have You Ever Taken a Stone?

Have you ever taken a stone,
A simple stone?

Rolled it in your fingers,
Clenched it in your palm,
Taking in its smoothness,
Its weight,
Opened your hand
And noticed its colour,
Thought of its history of presentient time?

Or perhaps you've bent over,
Scooped it up in your hand
With a clutch of others,
And sifted through them with your outstretched fingers,
Till it lay ready?

Ready to cast away,
To throw out into the free air,
To imagine a star-shot meteor,
A cannon roar from a galleon. No?

[...]

Perhaps you're practical then,
And have wanted to throw it away for no other reason,
Than ... ?

To watch it splash into water,
And slash out a tribe of ripples.
You might call them undulations,
Disturbances of surface tension ...

But I think you have missed it,
Much as we might miss swallows
In a rail yard of smoke,
Or the carnation in a well-dressed man's lapel

Think about it!
A little while,
at least.

You've got nothing to lose
But your impatience!

Mount Lawley,
2017

We Are Each Other's Voyeur

Was it Antonioni who said it all starts with a speck on the horizon ?

Our long sight reaches out in a desire to know,
and we patiently wait in space and time
for the revealing close up of a short-sighted face-to-face,
Which, if we read too abruptly,
blurs us into each other's eyes,
and demands speech or echoing breath to breath,
or a wrench away of the gaze to the floor,
or over the other's shoulder
as if they were not there.

Here now, then' I stand in recitation as a come-all-ye
or is it a tentative open mike?

[...]

I see you, yes you all -
a vast sea of expectation or cynical appraisal -
and I feel my loneliness
and my eyes seek out one of you
a recognisable 'you' to anchor down
the shift of space and time
to here, now, and this moment,
and you turn your head away to talk to the other beside you
and I return to lonely lost
as time expires
and I return to my place in the crowd
eyes to the floor.

What then the two of us
the furtive glance the sideways shift
the look to the lights above,
the slow lowering
to the straight line facing
and in that moment
warm acceptance or frozen rejection
with a sideways flick
that denies we were ever there.
Oh that we could rise together
face to face and enter each other
perhaps in body
or in spirit at least.
Mount Lawley
6 January 2017

One Reads of Songs

One reads of songs -
Like one's father telling of Nijinsky's dance -
One presumes, one judges and does not know.

Yet the words
Are not the music nor less the lyric,
Save they tell that you are not alone.
You who have worked solitary
In the dark passage of your twenty-four year mine,
And have brought so little ore to the surface.

It is like the desert
Which once you wandered in a hot cab,
Sweaty with man and dog,
And you knew that only 'you' and the heat
And that thing in the blood,
And though you passed camels ribbed in the sun,
You read no signposts of other hermits.

[...]

Yet in the gallow spinney of a great gum tree
Two travellers sprawled, tea pots, billies
And a faith that cool night would come.

So you must listen to the accounts of songs,
Watch even the vagrant sparrow sing
And learn that not only your tree sways the wind.

Perth Public Library
16 April 1959

Liza, Liza

Liza, Liza, ah hear yah knockin'
    Ah hear yah knockin'
        A knockin' at that porcelain door.

Ain't no use goin' in,
    They's just draggin the muddy river
        The dirty unwashed river
        The silt filled shambles

Shamblin' out old trumpets
    Blastin' up the neons, kid,
        Cuttin' rough with "Too close for Comfort"
    Baby doll is they for real?

Guy over there Liza,
    Yeah! the one with the cigar chompin' teeth,
    With those bugle boy eyes.
    Take him up the stairs.

[...]

PETER JEFFERY OAM

For how long?
        Come off it, dame; Just how long do you take?

        No, you can't have any beer up there,
        This ain't no lousy hotel.

        Lou, Liza's drunk.
        Drag her away from that toilet door!

Perenjori,
1957

River of Dreams

Liza, I hear you knockin'
A knockin' at that porcelain door
But there ain't no use in goin' in,
They'll just drag you back for more
So that dirty unwashed river
Of dreams will live on.

Shamblin' out 'ole trumpets
Blastin' up the neons, kid
Cuttin' rough, too close for comfort
Baby doll are they for real

Guy over there, Liza
Yeah the one with cigar chompin' teeth
Those bugle boy eyes will eat you up
Don't take them where they're longin' to be.

Liza, I hear you knockin'
A knockin' at that porcelain door
But there ain't no use in goin' in,
They'll just drag you back for more
So that dirty unwashed river
Of dreams will live on.

[...]

Now come on girl, Lisa
Just how long will you take
To realise there's no denying
Love just ain't no lousy hotel

Guy over there, Liza
Yeah the one with cigar chompin' teeth
Those bugle boy eyes will eat you up
Don't take them where they're longin' to be.

Liza, I hear you knockin'
A knockin' at that porcelain door
But there ain't no use in goin' in,
They'll just drag you back for more
So jump out of that river of dreams and move on.
So jump out of that river of dreams and move on.

Lyrics : Peter Jeffery.
Adapted for Music : Mike Greenacre 2020

Let's Get Going Now

Let's get going now
Let's get going now
Music gotta lonely time to run
Shorter than the sun
Longer than a breath
Baby let's just kick it to death
Let's get going now
Let's get going now

All the people want to stand and cry
Clap your hands and let it die
Let's get going now
Let's show the world how
The sea's only got five more waves to break
The earth's only got one more quake
But baby we're going Going to get going now
Baby let our hearts flower
Twirl our bodies and kick out our feet with power
Let's get going now.

Composition Upon Composition

As the teachers said in my early days
"Children colour in the squares!"
So I cover each
Note ~

What of the silences
Then?
The susurrus of unvoiced breath.
The rattle at the back of the dying throat?
No, rather
The purity of arrangement,
Spaces that
Augment and enhance,
Emblazon and condense,
Isolate and suture,
Spaces
That embed and hold and halt
Sound.

[...]

Solitary ~
Signal as a vertical spear
On an empty endless plain ~
Alphabets of phonic clusters
Die away in aboriginal deserts
To three, two, one voice.

Criss cross cutting,
Music among metal spheres,
Computers "talk up"

As with
The effluence riverine,
Coastal bays, mingling oceans,
The jargon of tools and trade,
Formulas of social forms,
Made cultures
Fragment and liquid And fluid
As music surging through
Pitch, volume, rhythm,
Staccato as the cicada of a Zulu click,
Or toning down meaning in Mandarin ~
Ma or ma or ma ; horse or dog or mother.

[...]

Webern then!
To this point.
Fragments of music, -
An archaeology of sound
Laid like shards on a table ~
Swelling into being,
Or fading into nostalgia -
Melancholy.

His orchestra then ~
A surgeon's plate
Of syringe, scalpel, clamp,
Spatula, clip, caliper ~
Where instruments of single sound
From string, skin, shell, wood
Resin, brass, stone, plectrum

Catgut, horsehair, steel.
Wind and water.
All merge into
Haphazard
Pattern
Of cultures,
Halls, plazas, arenas
Temples, cathedrals, Boudoirs, Mausoleums,
From Shepherd's flute, Soldier's drum -
Silvered castrati.

[...]

A GENERAL MUCH TIRED OF WAR

Fragments that flesh,
Fall away,
Show their raw raking,
Or in deep orchestra,
Concealed to all but the inner ear.

and still,
      Ever still,
           The silence
Of eternal possibility.

Composed on hearing Webern opus 28 string quartet Edith Cowan Conference on Poetry and Music

Eye to Eye

Twenty million of us here -
Flickering thoughts ever near -
And gone in a flash,
So let's all of us dash
Into the free fall conga.

You can lead,
If you need
Or let it all pass.

Arse following Arse
In the endless free fall,
That, too, for us all
Must surely come to pass.

Mount Lawley
18 October 2019

The Sea Is Not Small in Love

The Sea Is Not Small In Love
For Griffith Watkins

With due libation
for the life you gave to me,
in sad celebration,
I turn again to the sea.

I

Lapped cold by the North Sea,
burrowed back into a craven humility,
I could not stand to shout down grief,
jut my chest against Death's chill blast,
when they sent couriers
through the sea, through leaden cables they brought news
to me
of your death, lapped warm in the Swan,
drifting in circles about the last anchor
of your hopes, wry bitten off smile
laughing out the ever-bright eyes,
held in with crows' feet of suffering and sorrow.

[...]

Yet off Iceland's shore,
whelmed by wave and pitched
from foundering boat
a floundering man lay
as docile as me,
and emerged three days more from the sea.
My hopes for you
were as supine as this -
that dormant like Hardy's Troy,
shabby even, riding the circus hack,
you would burst in virility
and claim your own
treasures of praise and love.
The old red fox with busky tail
outfoxing us all with his deceptive tale.

[...]

A GENERAL MUCH TIRED OF WAR

But no,
much more desperate than that
you fled past all mothers, all lovers
into the warmest haven
the liquid blackness
that chills us, torn from the womb
thinking such retreat
a limbo tomb,
yet no less true,
for our endurance exhausts
and casts us into
fretful sleep,
as Shakespeare's cabin boy
lost aloft in the sails,
shrouded in fitful sleep.

In that sea of blood
we swirled in gentle peace,
our bodies compounded
with swimmer's perfect muscles,
to surf us out,
roaring through breakers of light
onto the world's final shore.

[...]

Your hope -

Not harmful, gentle child -
that the strangest swirling patterns
would turn you in trancelike devotion
to that ever half-hoped hour,
which would fade and turn again,
so that the swirling tides
would rock you gently to sleep.

Dear boy,
where has all the tension gone
out into that nonsensical sea,
where all the waves
pretend to die,
then come rushing back
and spend
like great seals
floundering on the beach,
eyes moist, jaws aslobber
as if about to perish.

[...]

A GENERAL MUCH TIRED OF WAR

Then, the ripple of water
floods about them,
moistens the flippers,
the leathery skin eases out,
the great bags become suppleness,
and they turn out
to the great heads,
where the waves
carry them away
into a sporting paradise.

II

But we remain
and though you've slipped the net
we complain,
'Return, restrain, remain!'
and though the net widens,
with teeming thresh
of escaping life,
we hold such gay threads
that we think we hold you fast.

Drifting in sun
and pleasant complicity
of words hovering like gulls
over our future,
white pure hopes
gliding away in casual abandon.
(no, I did not see
the sharp beak, bead bright eye,
the sprawling claws)
trailing beer bottle and wine,
bobbing gaily on the euphoria,
I thrilled to your assertive words
about the yacht slipping past the lights
into open sea.

[...]

And bermudas and thin chest,
you twanged the rope like ecstatic Triton,
so I laughed at our absurd dreams
and believed your eagerness,
your courage, the simple dare of next step
beyond last step.
Wordheld
I ran with you
dripping wave and rolling surf,
down the last
Paul Bunyan breaker
the greatest loomer
into the green haven of Garden Island.
(if only we'd foundered
and lay there all our lives!).

But in this drift,
there lies a tension of premonition.
You would, if you could,
reach out and hold them at bay
for me.
'King!' you would say,
'Let's go out on the midnight air.
I'll take the riff.'
And combo-like we would slip
down tunes of friendship
into starry sunny confidence,
lost in the great jam session of hope.

[...]

So, to another day.
Sun at Graylands,
and children tumbling at your feet -
Gay Sauls before a piping Gamaliel
as D'Artagnan-like you thrust
the foil of mental arithmetic
straight into their gay proferred chests.
Rapid, quick, life breathless in a whirl

like Dervishes in their trusting ecstasy,
they loved your teaching
'to know was to be gay, gay, gay!'
'to me my very thought is an action'
and I rose and knew,
I'd learned that thing or two
that teaching is to live greatly.

Two things more
from your general store,
generosity and self-discipline.

[...]

A GENERAL MUCH TIRED OF WAR

Lost in the hills,
striding free,
knee beyond knee,
word beyond word,
you drive yourself
across the page,
laughing in your age
at those of us, in the younger stage.
Lungs flame,
stars drift across the brain,
legs like cords
burst into flame,
beneath the sun
of your harsh desire.
Self, you assert
against the sky.
Voice in agonised cry.
Stoic,
heroic,
old dog hanging back,

[...]

last in the young runners' pack,
but still,
striding free,
knee beyond knee,
word beyond word,
laughing in your age you
drive yourself
page beyond page.

III

To turn in that brief second
and fill the beggar's bowl,
or pass on into ever thickening night
and watch mankind fall away
sterile, hostile, unfriendly, unsupporting,
you chose the better way.

Gave support to
a friend with a blighted mind,
stumbling words thick lippedly
over the desert of his life.
No hope, jobs failed.
Long empty waiting in gardens
with roses red and dull
against the searing electric blossoms
in the battering, tottering brain.
Quiet piece of cracked bowl,
you watch crumble again and again,
but knowing the shape of such a man,
disregarding the slavering
shavings of dust
you build back up with unquestioning trust,

[...]

this married man, family man,
walking into the legacies of life
with a new inevitability.
A Greek vase where all the athletes win the prize.

Stranger now, darker night,
driving wilder than his words,
and sliding across the white line
he brings up a rocketing pessimism,
darker than the bitumen,
and the countering lights, blaring horns
held an anxious inevitable logic
as clear as a capitulation,
with a final dare,
against the bridge pylon.
You laughed down his foolishness,
and held yourself against the crash,
waiting until later than the last
to bring him back with your final cast,
so that you both sat sweat drenched,
the car turning back into kitten
purring between his sobs
of acceptance back into life.
His killer shoulders
Husked down the air of hope,
like a diver gone too far down,
too far, too long, too far.

[...]

In the tortoise shell of the sun dappled surface.
Bush fire, aerial dancer
aloft in the gums, leaping fifty-foot voids,
and lost in recording wonder

you are encircled in fiery haloes of disregard
but green branch in hand
you beat a path
in fiery sparks.
Word jagged above the sky,
world jagged beneath,
gold bright your courage
and more durable than coal.

IV

      The sea is not small in love, I thought.
      Nor ever was; my need to forget
         ferrying me out ...
Your poem lifts as a dew from grass.
         My wandering bluer than any eyes I've known,
         sea becoming sky and sky sea
         in the endless anonymity of my sailing ...
You shift to the silence where no sounds pass,
         the pitch of the dark water soothing me.
         No more my mind an extended conversation,
         but cleared away of words ...
Your image slides away from the glass.

Sea, colloidal mass,
vaster than any grief,
tears you from us,
floods the island of yourself
with a conflagration
so abrupt
our boats of love could not come.

                                                [...]

A GENERAL MUCH TIRED OF WAR

In some seas shining surfs,
run to golden sands,
crystal springs
break against
the green rush of trees,
Villagers dance
in a crush of feet
beneath clear moon
and boats run to each
island the great chain
of friendship.

Yet in colder seas waves crash
on unyielding rock.
As curlews call
 against their
bracing shock.
You stand alone,
implacable stone,
and earn
our sad respect.

[...]

Yet
we shall never forget
your 'loveliest' line
from Dumas and Monte Cristo
> 'When he again rose
> to the surface
> he was fully fifty paces
> from where he had first
> sunk'.

Dear friend,
gallant captain y
ou will ever rise
in the warming sun
of our loving memory.

A Cacaphony
of Poets. . .

Over the Slabs of Meat
Occasioned by a poetry contest between Sheila, Don and myself

Over the slabs of meat, laid out square and neat,
I look through the glass and poster paint.
Then back to the sawdust floor
Over the wooden block, slashed a thousand times
The bounding half-skinned rabbit
Slammed against my boots and slid rubbery away
A rabbit of viscous flesh unlike that furry leveret.

Snow-white in the Christmas snow of a year ago.
And half kicked, half squashed,
Half carried on my boot I leave. Rather!
I would track a full fleshed stag
Antlering the centre of the road,
And clambering on its back, leave
Flesh behind, and ride into the celestial sky.

Mixing it at Matt's

A one o'clock start and no-one's there,
But like some errant stream of lava flow
The day hots up, steadily, and people singly weave
Through the accumulating cars,
And end up in a pool on the narrow veranda.
I arrive and sit near the only woman,
Who tells me that the other have been embroiled In a
philosophy liquor klatsch about the Void,
And what to do or not to do, regardingly regardless,
While she sips from her jar of vegetable juice,
Then devastatingly quotes from Omar Khayam -
All their problems resolved two centuries before!

I have come to hear the bands and the promise
Of a musical mayhem, and though I leave
When a single guitarist is hammering the floor,
And a female artist undulates like old Egypt,
And a long-haired ecstatic thrashes his hair,
Blurring into a constant inflow-outflow, demented,
The first two hours have pushed the spoken word
Through the open-mike and the clouds of ganja,
And even I, in part envy or ego thirst,
Read a rap and rant piece from years before,
Before I sober us all with my sister's elegy.

[...]

A GENERAL MUCH TIRED OF WAR

Unlike the MOON in its usual drowsy summer swoon,
The readers and chanters have woven the magic circle
Of intensity where ego rises and flattens

Into the equality of good conversation and brother and
sisterhood.
Body movement is the 'all' with Brillo and Boyd
As they do the half pivot and genuflect to the floor,
A single tapping drum measures heart beat,
Slow and wild, soft and loud, our heads nodding in time.
Poem retold, so how many times should we hear the
piece?
With Boyd's odyssey of time and place,
This is his best time yet, the repeat makes 'perfect'.

Matt takes the floor in a quieter buffer,
Talks of the Augustans like Pope
Then half ruminates as extempore
He slashes out with dry wit at the futility
Of a workplace romance, and we wince with him.

[...]

And so the day moves to night,
And, I am told, even beyond,
Casting the proposed curfew for neighbourly peace aside.
Yes, there's a lot of rant and rave,
Grand Prix speed and punk dissonance,
But cast against Boyd's epiphany
Comes another magic moment of stillness,
When one tall lady changes gender and our poetic time,
To court another blond, generous and beautiful,
And leads Brillo to bend and kiss her head.
Torn away, then, by commitment,
I would have loved to stay until dawn,
But I hope for a next time

Where one mixes it at Matt's
Mixes drinks, mixes styles, mixes sounds
And we once again hold our voices and hands
In that magic circle of poetry.

Mount Lawley
November 2015

A Coruscating Corona
For Coral Carter

Star turn at Matt and Craig's jam session,
reaches out daily to the clouds,
finds crucifixes everywhere
in churches and many irreligious places,
is almost strangled with her football scarves,
and along with Jenny she whistle stops Kiwi land
wowing them in every town,
crosses the border and drowns in family,
is the Kal-gal at ease wherever,
never forgets Woman's day with her huge post out of cards,
prints poet's dreams and anthologises the Moon,
and has her own book in Melbourne's Mainly Books,
her dresses a daily surprise   offbeat, colourful,
known in a thousand places for her endless graces.

[...]

But for me,
she is the saviour of our poetry festival,
when it seemed to be fading into burble,
and her wonderful early poem of a Chinese wedding bed,
all luscious and erotic in red and old
and occasion for a bi-cultural duel
with her Chinese interpreter-informer,
and most of all the sharp witness
of the bizarre in ordinary lives
and the ordinariness of the bizarre,
and the dignity of the poor and little
and humble people,
showing us as how we are
and not how we imagine ourselves to be.

So never fear Coral,
true guardian of the word,
you will be forever in my pantheon.

Mount Lawley
8 February 2017

A Coruscating Corona
For Coral Carter

Star turn at Matt and Craig's jam session,
reaches out daily to the clouds,
finds crucifixes everywhere
in churches and many irreligious places,
is almost strangled with her football scarves,
and along with Jenny she whistle stops Kiwi land
wowing them in every town,
crosses the border and drowns in family,
is the Kal-gal at ease wherever,
never forgets Woman's day with her huge post out of cards,
prints poet's dreams and anthologises the Moon,
and has her own book in Melbourne's Mainly Books,
her dresses a daily surprise   offbeat, colourful,
known in a thousand places for her endless graces.

[...]

But for me,
she is the saviour of our poetry festival,
when it seemed to be fading into burble,
and her wonderful early poem of a Chinese wedding bed,
all luscious and erotic in red and old
and occasion for a bi-cultural duel
with her Chinese interpreter-informer,
and most of all the sharp witness
of the bizarre in ordinary lives
and the ordinariness of the bizarre,
and the dignity of the poor and little
and humble people,
showing us as how we are
and not how we imagine ourselves to be.

So never fear Coral,
true guardian of the word,
you will be forever in my pantheon.

Mount Lawley
8 February 2017

"I Thought You'd Brought Some More Poems"
For Chris and Rose

If most gesture is tentative,
Like the wheat stem bending around and under rocks
It is only so that it grows the straighter
To its best and upright stance.
       With children tumbling in our hair,
Our visit then.
Led this way and that by the channelling screens
To admire objects delicately intrusive
An art-nouveau flower that is both iron and fey.
That is balustrade yet flowing imaginary.
       All this enjoyed,
Stronger things then;
Orwell's man bathed in pit-pony stance by his drab loving wife.
His photos of coal pickers lost in smouldering impotence,
Talk of cruelty and pain,
And taste of lemon hard on celery.

       So I interweave the joyous and dying afternoon
Into the strands of my brain,
To show you friendship
And a new poem, again.

Sunderland 9 April 1969

A SAD CAFE

We had a café, a sad café, where people came to cry
We had a negro trumpet, and Sorrow was his name.
We had eight tables, twisted and lined like a face in tears.

The music was a lost child's soul
Weeping the veil of night,
And the food was bittersweet
Spiced with sourish wine.

They crucified an artist here, on the thorns of their tongues,
Cut vertical gashes across the texture of his art,
Disfigured his name and naïve hopes with jealous words.

The pictures were twisted mazes of emotion
Drawn in frenzied lines,
And the candles were the stars of heaven
Spluttering on the earthly filth.

Perth

Jazz Piano in a Fernleafed Nightclub

Soft slow railyards of sound weeping out the wax on candles,
And the twinkling glass of crystalled keys,
All these, the piano of that doleful musicman,
Drinking out stars of love and blues
From a stained glass and chewed cigarettes.

We sit there, you and I watching,
Watching the shadowy spider web of hair mist your face,
And the little pine trees of shading creeping my face,
And our words are little sobs of sorry acceptance.

Then you see an errant flicker of the glad times
And you seize my hand and lead me,
Lead me out on the fernleafed floor,
And our tired feet with sad shoes scutter away the sadnesses.

Comes the slow taxi crawl up the canyoned street
And the light spilling doorstep and the steady kiss,
And the door closes and you clamber into your soft bed aching,
And I walk the cigaretted street home
Watching cars spray fresh water over dust drenched heart.

Perth, January 1957

PETER JEFFERY OAM

Where I'm From

Just West from Perth,
North of Antarctica -
Away from the laneways
That the night-cart trundled -
To that sunken bomb shelter
Erected in silence by the two mutes -
One my father - as neighbours.
All for our two hearing families to descend into
At the siren's roar that moved them not,
Until the flare of searchlights
Warns them, too, into hasty descent.

My strange street Janet, not Daphne,
But across Charles and my mother's name, Violet,
And in memory I see the billy cart,
Ball bearings swirling down to the highway, Charles,
But swerving to a halt in a retarding circle.
And by me my father passes with sawdust in his hair,
And on his back in hessian,
Wood cuttings for the laundry copper,
Or for me to assemble as cities and long trains,
Wooden not metal like the thumping pistons
And hissing steam that are
The test driven engines my Grandad drove.

North Perth Lesser Town Hall 2019

- Marina -

To Margaret

PART 1
"THE FACES OF LOVE"

Through the eternity of human permutation,
Love - a Hindu god in stone frieze,
changing appearance each drifted second -
revealed its many faces.

Each epiphany,
a flaming of the heart in unbearable light,
so that the body twisted thorned in delight.
      The delight in natural things,
so that I could say, with smiles and no embarrassment,
"Lately I have been in the habit
of holding flowers in my hand."
      The delight in musical strings,
leaping my parapetting mind
into steeples of celestial sound,
pouring sweet liquidity of song
over a darkened hovering of larks.
So high in my love,
that hawks fell below me,
that clouds were white pebbles,
and the stars
      fugitive firepoints from the furnace of my heart.
                                                   [...]

Ecstasy lasts no longer than the evaporating wine-drop;
and Lucifer-bound in
the finery of my pride,
I span like a feathered stone
down the wind-hall draughts of pessimism -
darkling the shattered hope, I, -
the fugitive wingbeats traced in pulp on pavements.

Each time like an essaying knight
with bone farced horse, gaunt and fear eyed,
and the dusty
white armour bent under the constant onslaughts
of jousting reality.
Each time,
the troubadour wandering out of anguish
in fine sounds.
Each time ...
   each time ...
     each time!

[...]

A GENERAL MUCH TIRED OF WAR

Then lust as plain as sword on velvet,
sharp and needlebright;
jettisoning ideals to make the scabbard
lighter, smoother, unchecked!
The blade of desire fire sharp,
plucking away the modest strands of hair,
merging to the hilt,
tumbling darkness in upon itself,
pulling down the fleshy folds,
till it lay
appeased!

Appeased,

but as pigs are appeased!
The swill empty, the rooting shapes
somnolent in the marshes,
husking away the exhaustion of satisfaction
to rise small eyed and snouting,
searching out the humid smell, -
      the piscine scent of further gluttonies.

The sad walking into the hills!

                                        [...]

The churches like skeletoned halls,
priests strangers! No, more enemies to be avoided!
Marys to be smiled at ruefully,
as if the supplicant was not praying
but tossing his head like a jester's cap,
the bells ringing, the eyes expectant
of mirth, but quietly understanding
the incomprehension of his audience.
The quiet retreat,
        ... the taking up of books,
                              ... the dereliction of hope.

The final settling in of the studied calculation,
the lack of involvement, the simulation of interest
which lay no deeper than friendship,
but was expected to be that of a lover.

        I watched her in a bed
while she had 'flu
and above her head
a shelf of glass animals
as sophisticated as brandy glasses
held in two hands and breathed from.
        I spoke,
      joked,
           even held her hand,
but it was most like visiting an old lady
of whom you'd slowly grown fond.

                                    [...]

A GENERAL MUCH TIRED OF WAR

I had cast a handful of seeds
that scattered in stuntling growths,
like the parables of Christ on ignorant peasant ears,
and I walked through
a tapestried forest of the unrealised,
where hope seemed finally unavailing,
till in the sudden flash,
       the Gogh sunflower,
          the fury throated fire of snapdragon,
I stood transfixed with your firmer growth.

No more wandering, now.
All past blooms express this most central fact

PART 2
"THE SEA OF ABSENCE"

I

Like the awakening of love
when the lids hover above recognition,
the water in tented tons, hung,
then smashed into spray,
tossing veils as high as aspirant hope,
or ran whiplashes of foam
along the raw rocks' edge.

We sat watching the endless sea,
the motion of its waves,
the scourling stone with its filigree of rock pools,
and crabs running like moisture from wet boots.
And in that instant we turned,
inward, onward, into
that blue ocean that stretches beyond the eyes.
Our hands entwined, our lips closed,
the thundering in our blood
more fierce than the drumming
bobbin threads of waves;
the spray tears on our bodies.

[...]

A GENERAL MUCH TIRED OF WAR

Time shifted, as endless as the windy hourglass of dunes.
We walked the strand,
our feet tracing odysseys behind us,
to be obscured into myth
and the faded images of a forgotten tribe.

Until we came to a hollow,
curled as God's own hand,
and silent, like dying string on a still night.
Sinking into its bliss,
our voices choired whispers,
as if two gulls skimmed across the sky,
plucking the plosive air in wingbeaten counterpoint.

Our words on absence were the spindrift of smoke.

I smile now at the words we spoke,
for even as they formed
I dreamed of love,
firmer than any betrayal of flesh
stronger than any eloquence of tongue,
and this would persist
would not decay
nor grow weak,
but would flourish
though sedge wither and suns go molten in the sea.

[...]

PETER JEFFERY OAM

In the ceramic of our heart's sky,
clouds hung with laughter
and we walked in chapelled peace,
the sea stretching away in glass.

II

In the harbour, the vessel turned,
an elephant, half swinging, half lurching,
its ponderous shape to the marking time of feet
while the frozen rain of ribbons broke,
showering the wharf and sides with sorrow.

I report only the sensations -
How can I speak the acid of tears,
the proud approval of waving hands
while the heart cowered in the haunt
of my eyes, making dark thunder?

The sun was warm;
        the sun was warm;
                the sun was warm!

The engine throbbed catlike,
as my voice laughed destiny,
"We've done it now!"
and I thought the silos on the horizon as white as Rome.

[...]

I had only sensations
like the taste of salt,
the sight of weed,
scent of oil,
touch of heat,
and sound of waves.
And I went down into the cabin and sighed.

PART 3
"THE LESSONS OF THE TIDE"

Marina ...
Forever the sea.
Marina ...
Forever the waves.
Marina ...
Forever the deeps.
Marina ...
    Marina ...
        Marina ...

Forever the sea sweeps our shores.
The blood is tides within the frame.

The shore of our lives
marks our phases;
from that first encroachment of weed
on the blank sunscoured sands of infancy,
through the longest clutching finger of foam
encompassing the foot,
to that retreat of age
which leaves its driftwood detritus
of tired experience and wrecked hopes.

                                        [...]

The sea is echoes in the blood.
Since that first heaving amphibian
lay on the warm shoals,
the shores of gold glazing its pale eye,
the surge has been forwards
through those steam drenched swamps
across vain deserts of dinosaur death,
beneath the impressing seas of ice
to this time of ours.

The sea is night in flood.

We act through time
as we move through water,
the lift and pull of the motive force
draws us inexorably to our end.

Time -
That suspended movement of motes -
swirls,
as the sea,
into the egress and bays
of Circumstance's complex shores.
Yet,
the movement of the tides

[...]

draws,
            withdraws,
                        draws
out the eventual meaning of life.
"For soon my child,
will all the mountains melt into the sea,
and the world be delta flats -
a hollow dancing of windy words
across deserts and dying weeds."

And such tides
brought strange shells and lessons
and shaped my life
as they have shaped boats,
from the first spinning coracle
to the metal fish that carved up Polar wastes.

I

We sang the Welsh countryside away,
the car corridored fields, meadows, churches,
hostels away into an endless frieze,
so that one expected white ducks and milkmaids;
not the stark skeletal town.
        A spinney with shattered arms
expostulated against the sky
at the sudden betrayal of the caves,
where only the shabby pit-horse of silence
stamps the galleys.
        Overcome by the resolute attack of flowers,
the heap of black waste
makes the deserted mine
into a jungle city
lost under the celebrant smothering of creepers.
        The town was the cemetery;
a blank series of white dabs
set in paths as crazy as grief.

        Life deserts certain cliffs,
so that shells seem fantastic on inland sands.
Without you,
I am that deserted cave
where ghosts staunch their departed hearts.
Yet in the faint breeze of your letters
I still remember flowers
on the mound of departed days.

II

This suburban church was as simple as a crib,
as ornate as hanging crucifix,
pendant jewel of sorrow on dark grained wood.
       It was the brooding eagle,
the palm crosses in children's hands,
the resolute timbers of Jacobean pews
to the adulterous and chaste,
       honest and corrupt,
         martyrs and persecutors -
the marching bands of Time.
       It was the splendid ruffles
on an Elizabethan arm,
or the rolling voice
of a Wesley before mobs,
quelling their murderous hate
into rousing choirs of song.
       For in the blood are the echoes -
the welling of ancestral sound
that dies in the corridor of the ears.
       It made clear an absence in the blood,

[...]

flooding with a respect and knowing,
those accretions of time that made my personal cliff
to buttress and stand in the waves of time.
      Such an absence have I felt,
in heath wandering days,
with trees gallows in the mood
and lovers and policemen stalking the maudlin dusk,
for you and the epiphany
of our interwoven trek of time.

A GENERAL MUCH TIRED OF WAR

III

      Five trolls fought with studded clubs,
and when their final hulks
cast up bony saplings on the hills,
the hollows flooded into lochs
from the silver tears of sky maidens.
      Out of dreamtime, the lake stands now
past the age when Romans shivered their armour
and swallowed down thoughts of Mediterranean Rome,
past the Vikings scrambling the forts,
their hills throwing up carousing halls and blonde children
from the fury of their conquest,
until the runes stood unspeaking;
while clansmen blew mournful pibroches
and herded shaggy beasts with doleful eyes,
to the Covenant flag
tattered, unstirred by winds,
until myself now.
      Until myself now
digging beans in a field with a crofter,

[...]

listening to talk of deer
and thinking of a mired helmet
lifted high by resurrecting shovel;
the loch beneath and cold as ice
anonymous in its time.

      It was as if I stood
on the scantling of time,
where rivers of past and future
receded on either Mosaic hand.
          A patriarch in our love
I have taken the tablets from these hills
and see the ordinance of our love
proscribed in their temporal covenant.

PART 4
"THE SACRAMENT OF RETURN"

I

Inexorably the sea moved,
her tons of water pounding the beach
with incessant artillery,
so that explosions of weed belched forth
and shells turned into wedding rings of bone
and gulls feet daintily danced among jelly fish.
      Then the long grudging retreat
leaving her battle lines scoured in sand,
while pelicans hold their beaks down in oceanic sleep
and pondered the peace of the depths;
and the moon exerted her strange command,
so that trains of sand swirled in velvets,
rays ghosted their diamond shapes
and squids feasted on gem like prawns;
and the sun, a strange observer,
with its bloodied eye of dusk,
and birds dropping like ashes in its beams
to silhouette and smash sparks
from the lighted trails of water.
      Thus the sea moved as it always moved.

[...]

PETER JEFFERY OAM

The body is that fish
that scrambled ashore,
and in the thousand day of God's time
became another thing,
until the lemming call of suicide
called the swimmer back
to swim the final stroke into a welcoming sea.

We who loved by the sea
returned to the sea
drawn by this sacrament,
this anniversary of wind and water.

A GENERAL MUCH TIRED OF WAR

II

The train lilted its trill of smoke,
gay streamer past this slumland pier,
to the beauty of the sea and green parks
with periwinkle bandsmen puffing in hot rotundas,
or in this more desolate time,
the mockery of ice cream cartons against the creaming
tides.

The captain puffing contented
in the security of his outstretched nets
drying in the flying wind,
turns to me and refuses my proffered hand,
my offered task to ride that bucking sea.
The land stretches round us like a cradle's sheets
and the sea is white wraiths of spray
beckoning even sirens to their death.

He is not afraid
the shark's pull, the confused weed in screw,

the gulls screaming beneath the sea hawk's talons
cruel beak pecking into sighting spheres
blotting out three suns;
earth - sight - life.

[...]

But that is in the sunlight
the honest sweep of light and wave,
the balance of blue sky and green water,
the sphere known, the environment of known terror
challenged each fish hauled day.

Now the sky is misted with its rumblings,
clouds clash with the waves
spray sprouts the fearful fingers,
and lightning jags the day in portent
of cauldroned and certain death.

Our talk wages its own elemental war,
my will trying to prise the clamshell of his mind apart,
to insert the grainy pearl of your onetime words.
Sudden the sky plateaus its clouds and silver gilds the
   grey,
and his eyes relax their vision of death
and audacious certainty measures our stride to the beach.
Upon his confidence,
he is Neptune again in the power of his trident,
gulls feather and flute their attendance,

But I would welcome the finny death,
the scales of shimmered water about my eyes,
the gulps of that ocean without
and within my watery blood.

[...]

A GENERAL MUCH TIRED OF WAR

The boat bucks her cortege way
through the respecting waves,
clutching their wailing wakes
about her coffined form.
The captain is words and fury with the wind,
his hands wrestle the wheel,
the spray showers his coat,
as the salt tightens his beard.
He is alive
crying his Promethean yell from the stake
of his ship,
against the storm's chains
that binds his defiance to the realm of rocks,
weeds, and reefs.

I am dead.
Your ashes in my pocket
bear the last seed of hope.

Dejection entraps my soul.
The turtle soup tureen of salty waves, uncertain weed,
echo the mood, as I watch
the long line of white
marking the timeline of our shared life.
And then, like that embered dove,
I renew my hope in the memory of our young love.

[...]

All Adam and Eve as the Welshman said,
all pure as that clear sac near the newborn lamb,
all Rousseau with the timid lions and misted shapes,

all Darien and unique as we climbed that mutual peak.
And just as salt must be in bread,
this existence is understood.

The ocean is new. It is all love,
meaningless with the consistency
of a wave's changing pattern,
necessary as the myriad plankton
was to that albino whale,
effluxing the greatest sorrow of man on twisting cross,
driving the shoals forward and back under the migrant
sun.
Love is existence -
is the slow retreat of steps into enshrouded dunes,
or the tattered steps that bubble a thousand
breaths beneath the killing effacing waves.

From this ocean, then, I haul
in the memories and tally them as children do shells
on a hardwood table.

[...]

A GENERAL MUCH TIRED OF WAR

In my Van Gogh boats
that once hung our lives,
was the peace of beached security.
> "I beach my boat on the white shores of your
> thigh,
> And my prow comes to rest in a black nest of
> waves."

And now as the boat makes her eventual circle,
I see this etched again on the sphere of our wake.

The engine chugs its pistons up and down,
a mechanised solider marking
the relentless time of my thoughts.

The ashes spill from my hand,
their dry shape sponging instantaneous water,
trailing a chaotic ribbon,
a bunting of a thousand flags,
a galaxy in the sea's stars,
a universe and an extension beyond,
a final ephemeral sea of ether
with no bounds, no meaning
but our love.

The sea is rough.

[...]

My eyes have gone beyond that mist of spray,
my grief beyond the cavern of my mouth,
my love beyond the grotto of my mind.
The captain smiles as he commands the heads
and runs down the long gullet of return.
He is master again before his winter's fire,
and his sons will ride the waves in this memory,
and he will talk his final night of how
he tossed the statue of the sea god overboard,
and no Cyclopean fear would haunt him.

For myself,
I see a trek into seclusion,

Characters

Characters

Flowers

Freed from school, his head bent to the pavement,
As he ran home avoiding the cracks,
He almost bumped into her, As she stood in his path,
Towering above him, adult to child.

She is arresting, arrests him
With the stab of her voice
The long pin in her hat.

'These bees are your friends' she says
Pointing up above them
Into a molten buzzing swarm

Stab of the sun,
Stab of the finger,
Stab of the sting!

[...]

Terrified he is held
In the ever widening lariat of her eyes
Until, dancing to one side,
He moves around her and away.
his feet thudding, his chest heaving
he looks behind
and she is a mottled Francesca
conversing and praying with birds and bees
 In later years he said
'Flowers' is what we called her

And remembers how her bonnet was all bright
Her dark dress moth-eaten, wild smell,
And how like a haphazard corsage
She trailed a basket of withered blooms.

North Perth State School.

Connections

Man dancing
Two girls dancing
Alone
Together
Myself
Moving to music
Stabbing out onto the floor
Eyes shut
Bowie hips pursed beneath beard
Disco
Spinning, drinking, smoking
Gays gay
Butchers looking at butches I peer through my lids
At the twirling kids
Sexual sensual
Potential
Climbing along the clarinet
Sprawling over the drums Scatter, snare
Bocardi and coked
Right up
Make up

[...]

What you will
Glitter gator
Hot potato
Old man
Dissolving into smoke
Revolving dervish
 Slightly pervish
Ever nervous
Night rushes cold across
The Northbridge pavement.
Wet from the late night sweepers.

Vision of Dreamtime

Walks weary
        Eyes bleary
                Sun flames dreary.
Till night crashes the skull,
And Death drifts slowly into his eyes.

The pool stretches oceans,
And emus stamp the earth like moas,
And wombats big as boulders stumble the track.
The earth is a golden feeding
And the trees are shading mats,
And flame spirals the sky.

A crow croaks
        Chokes
                Pokes

His beak in the soft flesh,
Sun slowly revealing the mesh
Of bones, which made thresh.

[...]

His body is a singing hut
Where winds mouth the branches.
The desert is soft as brolgas dancing
In the moon.
Giants wander among the stars,
And call him up.
He has left his hut and come.

Shifting Moods

Shifting Moods

Total Self Concern

The bowels move and the toilet, as bare as monastic cell,
Delightful as a suntrap becomes 'thunder box' and is heir
to all
My daily masticulation, and the odours hold
To go unremarked or the butt of jokes,
But as vaporous as the words on this page
And as substantial.

And a panic to both write and not write,
To be lost in a miasma of reading
Always to a purpose, and that is - not to arrive -
And to stop typing
Thus ...

My eyelids are heavy with flu,
Saturated in tablets and endlessly puffing
Through the plastic lungs of plastic cones, I
nverted and holding - a combust belly -
That holds breath away to allow deeper breath
To take and invade the lower belly.

Mount Lawley
31 May 1999

Soren Kierkegaard

The dread finality of weighty decision
Was borne lightly upon your back.
You Christed yourself in a world ignorant of Christs
And died denying the puppet rites of the State's Church.
I have sympathy for you
In the dereliction of your love
In the blind leaping of your faith
In the denial of all earthly things established;
But you died an unrich man.
Granted, you will revel in God's eternal Light.
Singing His praises all starry eternity,
But I say the decision once made
Is the knotted agony of a twisted cross,
And it seems flagellant to take pleasure in pain.
I would ratter a hermitage in the world,
And not in the icy wastes of the intellect,
Forever is the draught of life force to be drunk,
Ever is the sudden flash to be revealed,
And sometimes the errant pleasure is most permanent.

Perenjori
1957

Floating Fragments on my 23rd Birthday

It is my birthday - the day when my flesh cascaded into
the fiery light of Life -
and I am glad, for the earth -
though it has played the roles of matron, strumpet,
and lover to me -
is of itself good, like bread, or the barley in beer.

I have grown tall in the stature of the sun,
and though not given with the strength of young lions,
yet I am not sickerly, but sprite as a sapling is to breeze.

I revel in the joy of being -
in that accomplishment of existence,
that no dead sage can diminish -
for my life is like a plume half scrawled across a page,
with journals more to traverse.
I am twenty three; and the day is full of sweet promise.

SS.TOSCANA
15 January 1958

Indian Summer

Man that is born of a woman is of a few days and full of trouble.
Lo, he cometh forth like a flower, and is cut down ......

      He looked, and was pleased with what he saw
The trees were alive with the fighting life of green,
and the corn stood high and rich
against the pastures, lush with sudden growth,
and the dugs of his mare hung heavily
with the promise of life.
      The air was sweet with scent of flowering
      stream,
and rich soil, black and damp -
and the earth crunched beneath the boot.

      The first arrow hit him in the throat.
The second tore into the flesh below the left lung
and snapped, as he stumbled to the ground,
and his body twitched like a cut worm.
They burnt the maize; rose a mountain of red
against the evening sky,
and that night, the mare ate of forest grass.
The air was rank with tart smoke
and the stench of ash stained pine,
and the earth swished beneath the mocassined feet.
Perth.

The Refugees

And they came down into Egypt;
She, the Woman, bent with child,
And the little ass plodding in desert dust,
And the carpenter, bridle rope acid in his gnarled hand.

Behind rode the squadron of armour,
Cursing the sand sea, and the sear heat
Sucking, like spavined calf, at Earth's sterile teat,
And they thought often of the slave girls,
And rolling dice, and rosy flesh, and necklets of pearls.
The captain had sneered at the shuffle foot priest,
The witch woman, and the stutter-oracle, all attendant
upon the king,
But now he rode, like sweat mouthed beast,
A demon flooding his ears; the voice of his king.

And they came to an inn,
Warm with life and moving life,
But the keeper came to the gate, his bleary head shaking,
And they shuffled off - silent suffering.

[...]

That night the cavalry commandeered the inn;
The wine flowed free as bubbling spring,
Rich red, thick as blood, and peasant girls dancing
In the warmth of youth, and an old piper, toothless,
Haunting a rhythm of maiden and ancient kings ruthless.

The parents and young men had been torn
From their hostel-stable beds, and huddled against the wall,
Brooded impotent menace, or waited for the dawn;
Bearded oath, whining obedience, sounds against the wall.

And they came down into a dry valley,
Deathlike and sombre with rocks,
And the cactus, lonely in its hermit triumph,
And camel bones, singing in the wind.

The armour was hot on belly and thigh,
And the head a cracked water jug spilling with sound,
And the tongue, hard, dry, hanging as a hound's,
Yet they rode lightly now, armour jingling,
For in the distant heat, three spots were twinkling, tingling.
Flat dunes, long slow-soft curling waves,
And no shelter, no place to hide
But the rocks, cairns marking lone desert graves,
Where weird prophets or demented camel drivers have died.

A GENERAL MUCH TIRED OF WAR

And they came to ask of the desert shelter,
But the rocks stood haughty, smooth polished,
And the cactus laughed as it shook its spiny arms;
Only the humble sage hugged them with stringy limbs.

They searched long and patiently,
The short sword, peering like a cat, grazing cactus flesh,
And suddenly, a shattered snake threshed
Its life away, its blood blending red with he dust.
They rode away, the horses' rumps slowly swinging,
And their armour glinted with tarnished light,

And the carpenter and his wife came out singing,
And the ass knelt down and the sage was holy with halo light.

And they came down into Egypt;
She, the Woman, bent with child,
And the little ass plodding in desert dust,
And the carpenter, bridle rope acid in his gnarled hand.

Words This Way And That

Above the Cluttered Houses

Above the cluttered houses of Digbeth
The black stroke of a bird swirls
Forcefully like a leaf dictating
Its own seasons -
Ikon of the free spirit,
A lark above larks.
I am caught here in a city
Neither cold nor hot
For all its belching furnaces
Warm as pigeon shit.

In Birmingham with Stuart Hall
And despite the warm bread
Of his welcome that makes me brother,
Study and exile here is hardcoin.

But money is greeting - here the proffered price -
And then the greeting is paid for,
Despite the hypocritical, 'You're welcome.'

[...]

A GENERAL MUCH TIRED OF WAR

Gunfactories, auction yards, silent black canals
Edged by wild flaming flowers that sear one's eyes,
Swallowing all shades, green over crumpled tin,
Flapping wire and unwound winch.

Here, as if in a dream,
My son leaps for the surf,
On a washing machine lid

He swirls downhill on the one-day snow.

My entrapped eye reaches out
For the range, the run, the dry rumple line
Of the Australian horizon,
With the metaphysical blue of the ocean
Drained into an unself regarding emptiness -
The resolution of all entropy.

Free Fall

Ta write a poem
A man's gotta have words.
What about a woman?
Does she gotta have words,
Or is she
In free-fall,
Thisaway,
Thataway,
Anyway,
Noway.

Everything,
Everybody
Is in the free fall.
Falling free from time to time
Slow and fast,
Time present Time past.
Holds on tight
To things gone loose,
Aright,
Astray,
Awry
Both pretty and ugly,
Seen left eye
Right eye
Cross eye
Sunken eye,
Bulging eye

A Fragment Towards Kella!

More bright than sun, the water in her hand
Night was a bandage around her eyes,
Silence bathed her in its sound of rushing blood
The world was incomprehensible obstacles
She was to use a lamp as her symbol
That day was all the other days
The effort to communicate
A dog howls the moon with more success
The pump and the water like jewels
The onrush as with the epiphany of Pentecost
The falling into place of the water
The nervous squeals of pleasure
The frenetic hands

Journal De Jour – January 1

This Christmas break of 2016 then, with its reading and movies
all flowing together making meaning and dissolving into nonsense
And all of this in the fleshy folds of my brain,
Lit up like an electrical firework of display
Making a network of my sole thought
That makes my individual self totally social
In a enforced embedding manner
That renders this poem unique or common place
All at once and the same time.

Through the endless days
A myriad of images and objects and practices all impinging
In a visual virtual textual chronology ever shaping ideology
Of world views shifting in and out
Of solidity and vaporous transformations
Make my life the insuck and outpuff of breath.
So that with Buddha one thinks
All is illusion
Until that final moment for which there is Nirvana,
Kama, satori and/or endless emptiness.

                                                            [...]

And through all of this runs family concerns and feasts
Of risotto and turducken and ingestion and excretion and
Event and swirling dreams and the consumption of distance

Between on pump to the next.
The animation *Red Turtle* with its flippering flow of tsunami,
Sand dunes, the erotic Blue Lagoon turned mythic Japanese,
A cyclic rendition of the human condition,
Shifts to the text of a New Zealand history speaking of a Polynesian
Circular thousand-year eddy that invades the land of the Moa,
To the Pakaheh of invasion and unsettlement of the
Earlier network of mana, pa, and to become both rich and poor
Caught up in the Weltchmerz of European concerns
And the similar economic eddy of itinerant workers
Between islands and continent.

Every moment of sight and sound that navigates
Us between the jagged materiality of this world
And its semiotic is plethora
And leaves me swimming Until I drown and I feel
I could not and would not
Have it otherwise.

Trace, Track, Route, Root ...

Trace, track, route, root, shadow, outline, gaps, trail
Memory as words, images, places, people, scents,
Fade, shade, shadow, dimming, silhouette,

Vincent Street
Saint of raw pain,

Do we make a route, a map, a trap of memory?

Tribal survival,
Each part of the story holds building to building

The street as pageant as storied, storyed holes in rock
A hundred moments in parallel enactment
Al event, all performance, all passively still
Rising from shadow and fading, shading abrading,
Reading the world in to shaping meaning.

PETER JEFFERY OAM

Towards 'The Ides of March'

Sunday 1

Will I assault you dear friends
Just as you and the rest of us
Strangle each other with endless rosaries of Dies Irae,
Each to our fashion but oh so boringly predictable
Or shall I write
Day by day to the Ides of March,
Where in half love I embrace you with one arm
And with my lips to your side face,
Thrust the dagger with the other
Into your belly
Kerplunk - in the gizzard,
In ambitious betrayal.

[...]

A GENERAL MUCH TIRED OF WAR

Monday 2

On the verge of midnight
And searching the day
For a topic to ignite my steps towards the betrayal
Of the pulsating squirt of ink
That creates the necessary poem -
Foggy groggy smoggy soggy blog -
Sufficient to the day thereof.

Bubonic plague, Spanish flu, Chinese
We did not know that the dead were so many
That all things pass
But the earth abides, abides, abides

Before our birth, after our death,
Every trace that comes into being fades, fades
As ashes to ashes and dust to dust.

[...]

Tuesday 3

Tokyo Station, or is it Hanoi intersection?
Where the proof, of an event that makes History,
Is the crossover of Time and Location.

And so thus impelled we step into the flow and,
But for the lift of a foot, would be knocked sideways
And thrust down to the hard floor, be made instant island.

Above this maelstrom of people going to who knows where,
The marker of a clock, or further down at eye level,
The toilet once binary and now uni-gendered,
Gives us a target to achieve, for the other anonymous body
To meet by appointment, as if meaningful.

But more often our movement is mindless,
And we are rammed by a board across our backs
Into the interior of the carriage like sardines in the tin,
And woe betide us if we cannot escape at a prescribed station,
Like the man in the song about his journey on the circular route,
And the question. 'Oh! Will he ever return? Will he ever return.

ELEGY

ELEGY

I Would Not Have You Otherwise
For Daphne, Tina and family.

The morning is mourning black,
Though I am sunblasted in the long penitential walk,
My sweat refreshes me one last time
Prepares me for a final redeeming talk.

Words contrapuntally set in English and Greek
Interweave in deep chant song,
Echoing the shifting text of your Australian Greek life.

The walls are gold leafed and iconic with a pageant of saints
In this most colourful mortuary and ossuary,
The blinding brightness is held back
By the long lines of women in black

We have been summoned by the single peal of a bell,
Incense swirls around and past the coffin
Drenched in flowers
The susurrus of the swinging chains
Makes a metronome for our rosaries and worry beads.
Our tears skip like scattering rain over roses.

[...]

The priest calls up the comforting universal text,
And says yes the earthly body is dead but the soul
Is elsewhere, our Daphne has fallen asleep
In a field of flowers, past pain and sin and sense.
 Grief stricken and angry with the wrenching loss
A man leaps up and shouts in a heart-rending voice
'Daphne, tell us of Daphne!' refusing the calming message
For us all in the biblical text of redeeming Christ,
And hammers futilely on the church door.
I hear of Daphne's dramatic flair and smile ironically
For we have had drama more than enough here.

The priest returns to the resurrectional text briefly,
Then recounts that from this sleep there will be a judge-
ment
But from the compassionate Son of God
Where our life is reviewed temperately
Both for the pain and hurt and the love and kindness
We have done for others.

He then moves into eulogy and shows the life of Daphne
In its great heights and its lowest depths,
And emphasises her vivacity, her drama,
Her peace-making wisdom learnt from experience,
Her unique art turned by her generous heart
Into gifts to others without thought of career,
Or self-possession - all filled with the joy of making,
So many who knew her see her as a beautiful girl,
Gentler than most, more trusting, sweeter too.

We file out in the waiting cars that take us to Karrakatta
To the necropolis of the emigrant Greek community,
To her graveside, to the awning for the elderly,
The crumbling carpeted walkway over the slope
And final cast of earth or flower or special object,

And descend into the final sweetness of Delight
And the sharp bite of brandy or the cooling water,
But in the bus's long wending way I have seen errant
A pair of women's shoes, in among the leaves
And for me Daphne has walked

Away from all of this, and is waiting for me
To come and rest in easeful, laughing thoughtful talk
In the sun with our coffee outside her little home,
And talking of our next foray into Art.
And I am enchanted as she talks of Greece
And the three villages of her ancestors
And I glory that she has this and Paris too.

As I write this I have the Language of Flowers
By my side and its only entry for Daphne -
Its emotional meaning is this:
'I would not have you otherwise!'

Mount Lawley
December 2015

> # Acknowledgements

As the saying goes 'Art is long, and life is short', and the number of people who have supported me in the great game of Poetry has been legion, even in my short and fading eighty six years to Heaven.

www.ingramcontent.com/pod-product-compliance
Lightning Source LLC
Chambersburg PA
CBHW010245010526
44107CB00063B/2685